DAVID

ENDORSEMENTS

David: The Godly Heart of a Sinful Man is a classic read that gives incredible insight into the life of David. Using vivid imagery and practical application, this book paints the struggles and triumphs of a man who truly desired to serve God ... but let his flesh get the best of him. I would highly recommend this book for anyone who is looking for a closer, authentic walk with God.

Rusty Smith
Pastor, Mikado Baptist Church

Pastor Terry Hyman has ably articulated the power of a godly man, who was totally surrendered to the Lord. This book will challenge, motivate, and deepen your walk with the Lord. I can highly recommend it.

Evangelist Jerry Sivnksty

In his previous book, Pastor Hyman did an outstanding work in his study of the Minor Prophets. In his study *David: The Godly Heart of a Sinful Man*, he has done an equally masterful work. I was personally challenged! His writings are very beneficial to both pastors and laymen alike. Pastors will benefit greatly through his homiletics, and everyone is challenged to godliness. My prayer is that his books will have wide circulation.

Ron Comfort
Evangelist and Founder of Ambassador Baptist College

TERRY W. HYMAN

DAVID

THE GODLY HEART OF A SINFUL MAN

Ambassador International
Greenville, South Carolina & Belfast, Northern Ireland
www.ambassador-international.com

David
The Godly Heart of a Sinful Man
©2022 by Terry W. Hyman
All rights reserved

ISBN: 978-1-64960-031-8
eISBN: 978-1-64960-030-1

Cover Design by Hannah Linder Designs
Interior Typesetting by Dentelle Design

No part of this book may be used or reproduced in any manner whatsoever without written permission except in the case of brief quotations embodied in critical articles or reviews.

All Scripture quotations are taken from the King James Version of the Bible. Public Domain.

AMBASSADOR INTERNATIONAL
Emerald House
411 University Ridge, Suite B14
Greenville, SC 29601
United States
www.ambassador-international.com

AMBASSADOR BOOKS
The Mount
2 Woodstock Link
Belfast, BT6 8DD
Northern Ireland, United Kingdom
www.ambassadormedia.co.uk

The colophon is a trademark of Ambassador, a Christian publishing company.

For he remembered that they were but flesh ...

—Psalm 78:39a

TABLE OF CONTENTS

INTRODUCTION
  DAVID'S CHARACTER 9

CHAPTER 1
  DESTINED FOR THE PALACE 13

CHAPTER 2
  MUSIC FOR A SIN-SICK SOUL 21

CHAPTER 3
  STANDING TALL IN
  THE SHADOW OF A GIANT 27

CHAPTER 4
  WINNING SPIRITUAL BATTLES
  AND LOSING GROUND 37

CHAPTER 5
  THE FUGITIVE KING 47

CHAPTER 6
  IN THE COMPANY OF FOOLS 59

CHAPTER 7
  WAITING ON GOD 69

CHAPTER 8
  DAVID BECOMES KING 79

CHAPTER 9
A UNIFIED CROWN 87

CHAPTER 10
BRINGING THE ARK HOME 97

CHAPTER 11
WHEN KINGS GO FORTH TO BATTLE 107

CHAPTER 12
BASKING IN THE GOLDEN
GLOW OF SUCCESS 121

CHAPTER 13
DEALING WITH GUILT 129

CHAPTER 14
DAVID'S GODLY HEART 137

CONCLUSION
THE SOURCE OF GODLINESS 149

ENDNOTES 151
ABOUT THE AUTHOR 153

INTRODUCTION
DAVID'S CHARACTER

THE STORY OF DAVID IS the ultimate "unexpected success" story. An obscure shepherd boy from Bethlehem rose to become king of Israel. *Unqualified, undeserving,* and *unsuitable* are all words that man would use to describe this unlikely candidate for royalty, yet God does not reason like man. He saw something in David that made him worthy of divine attention. David's heart was different. David had a yearning to follow God, an eagerness to have God's blessing on his life, and a willingness to sacrifice when necessary. "A man after his own heart" is how the prophet Samuel described God's view of David in 1 Samuel 13:14.

Yet this "man after [God's] own heart" had feet of clay.

- How can it be that a man who said in Psalm 18:36, "Thou hast enlarged my steps under me, that my feet did not slip," failed to learn the steps necessary to successfully move the ark of God (1 Chron. 13)?
- How is it possible that a man whose heart was so concerned with pleasing his God that he could not bring himself to slay the anointed king of Israel in self-defense (1 Sam. 24:6) could be so bold as to ruthlessly murder one of his most dedicated soldiers to conceal a personal sin (2 Sam. 11:14–17)?

- What motivates a man who clearly understood that his authority came exclusively from the sovereign Creator of the universe (Ps. 8) to arrogantly number the people under his command (1 Chron. 21:1-7)?

David was a man of many contrasts. The tenderness of a gifted musician was paired with the toughness of a hardened soldier. The generosity of a gracious king was set off by the greed of a self-absorbed monarch. He was conscientious though impulsive, pensive though impatient. While his heart sought after God, his flesh often led him astray. In Psalm 119:10 David pleaded for God's help when he said, "With my whole heart have I sought thee: O let me not wander from thy commandments."

David's character is clearly revealed in Psalm 101. In verse two David said, "I will behave myself wisely in a perfect way. O when wilt thou come unto me? I will walk within my house with a perfect heart." While he failed to keep that pledge on many occasions, behaving wisely was a frequently acknowledged character trait in his life. Three times in 1 Samuel 18, David is said to have "behaved himself wisely" (vv. 5, 14, 30).

Perfection is an impossible standard to achieve for all humans, and David was no exception. Spurgeon noted, "David's resolve was excellent, but his practice did not fully tally with it. Alas! he was not always wise or perfect, but it was well that it was in his heart."[1] Those who plan to be perfect come closer than those who don't. While that doesn't excuse David's failures, it does reveal a very important aspect of his character.

People often ignore details when making general commitments, but in Psalm 101 David chose to identify three specific elements of his pledge:

1. *Wise behavior requires a solemn resolve to avoid the influence of wickedness.* "I will set no wicked thing before mine eyes" (v. 3). Implied in this statement is a decision not to desire, observe,

tolerate, or meditate on that which is wicked. When encountered unavoidably, a wicked thing is to be despised and abandoned.

2. *Wise behavior demands purity of motive and separation from those who are corrupt.* "A froward heart shall depart from me: I will not know a wicked person" (v. 4). Spurgeon characterized David's attitude this way: "He refers both to himself and to those round about him; he would neither be crooked in heart himself, nor employ persons of evil character in his house; if he found such in his court he would chase them away."[2]

3. *Wise behavior requires kindness toward neighbors and humility of spirit.* "Whoso privily slandereth his neighbour, him will I cut off: him that hath an high look and a proud heart will not I suffer" (v. 5). Pride and slander are close cousins. Those who hold positions of great authority often feel justified in disparaging the character of those beneath them. Doing so bolsters their image while destroying their victims. David knew from personal experience the pain and sorrow associated with such tactics.

David's goals were not too lofty—his humanity just got in his way, as it does with every individual. God did not choose him because he was a perfect man; He chose him because of the character of his heart. Not a perfect heart, but a heart that was tuned to God's voice, a godly heart—clothed in human flesh.

CHAPTER 1

DESTINED FOR THE PALACE

THE FIRST MENTION IN SCRIPTURE of David becoming king of Israel was not very grand—it did not even include his name. The announcement was not made at a ceremony called for that purpose, nor was the message broadcast publicly. The proclamation is found in 1 Samuel 13:14:

> But now thy kingdom shall not continue: the Lord hath sought him a man after his own heart, and the Lord hath commanded him to be captain over his people, because thou hast not kept that which the Lord commanded thee.

The announcement was made by the prophet Samuel to Saul, at that time the king of Israel, who had by his attitude and actions distanced himself from God's continued favor and blessing. David, the young shepherd boy to whom the announcement referred, was busy tending his sheep in a field outside Bethlehem. He had no idea what was happening or how dramatically his life was about to change.

The first mention of David's name in Scripture was likewise rather unimpressive. He was, after all, only a "sheep boy." The youngest son of Jesse of Bethlehem, he was held in much derision by his older brothers and considered to be of little assistance to the family other than tending their sheep. Even Jesse, his father, had little respect for the abilities and contributions of his youngest son. He was obviously unaware of David's courage and skill.

To be fair, shepherding in those days would not be listed as one of the most sought-after professions in Israel. Working conditions were often harsh, requiring the shepherd to endure scorching heat during the day and frigid cold at night. Jacob repeatedly endured such conditions while tending sheep for his father-in-law, Laban. In Genesis 31:40 he described his adversity: "In the day the drought consumed me, and the frost by night; and my sleep departed from mine eyes." Shepherding was not an easy job, and there were few volunteers. Consequently, responsibility for the sheep was generally relegated to the youngest son in the family.

While faithfully tending those sheep one day, David was summoned to a meeting in Bethlehem. The prophet Samuel was there, along with his father and seven older brothers. They were preparing to enjoy a feast celebrating the sacrifice that was a pretense for Samuel's visit (1 Sam. 16:5).

Samuel had already interviewed David's older brothers. But God made it clear that His choice was not yet in the room. Had it been left up to Samuel, Eliab, the eldest, would have been the next king of Israel (vv. 6–10). Somehow Samuel had a problem discerning character. In one of his greatest errors, he had failed to see the deviant character of his own sons, making them judges over Israel (1 Sam. 8:1–3).

In this case, however, God intervened, making it clear that Samuel was using the wrong benchmarks to make his choice. God's criteria had more to do with the character of the individual being considered than his outward, physical appearance. After all, God had said that His choice, already made, was a "man after his own heart."

What happened next must have seemed strange to David. First Samuel 16:13 gives us the details:

> Then Samuel took the horn of oil, and anointed him in the midst of his brethren: and the Spirit of the Lord came upon David from that day forward.

Then Samuel left. There was no ceremony, no announcement. Samuel simply did what he came to do and left.

We have no indication of David's initial reaction to what had just occurred. There is no question that he understood the significance of the anointing, but at least for a while, nothing changed in his life. He simply returned to the sheep. *The newly anointed king of Israel continued to tend sheep.* It would, in fact, be many years before David actually assumed first the throne of Judah, then finally the throne of a united Israel.

MAN'S DESIRE—GOD'S PURPOSE

David's anointing came at a time when Saul, the first king of Israel, was still on the throne. Saul and David were alike in many ways. Both were extremely popular with the people of Israel. Both were fearless soldiers who excelled in battle. Both had abundant leadership qualities and garnered great respect from their followers. Both also engaged in sinful activities that threatened to remove them from power. There was, however, one significant difference: Saul was concerned with his power and prestige, while David was consumed with a desire to please God.

Saul became king because the people demanded a king. Their desire was not weakened though Samuel warned of the Lord's disapproval, nor were they dissuaded by his detailed description of oppression and hardship associated with being subjects of a king. Samuel's prophecy was indeed sobering:

> Samuel told all the words of the Lord unto the people that asked of him a king. And he said, This will be the manner of the king that shall reign over you: He will take your sons, and appoint them for himself, for his chariots, and to be his horsemen; and some shall run before his chariots. And he will appoint him captains over thousands, and captains over fifties;

and will set them to ear his ground, and to reap his harvest, and to make his instruments of war, and instruments of his chariots. And he will take your daughters to be confectionaries, and to be cooks, and to be bakers. And he will take your fields, and your vineyards, and your oliveyards, even the best of them, and give them to his servants. And he will take the tenth of your seed, and of your vineyards, and give to his officers, and to his servants. And he will take your menservants, and your maidservants, and your goodliest young men, and your asses, and put them to his work. He will take the tenth of your sheep: and ye shall be his servants. And ye shall cry out in that day because of your king which ye shall have chosen you; and the Lord will not hear you in that day. (1 Sam. 8:10-18)

Law, when administered by men who are driven by power and greed, always devolves into tyranny. Israel simply wanted to be "like all the nations" (v. 5). Saul was, in essence, man's choice, not God's.

The new king's reign, however, was plagued by scandal. Saul's persistent disobedience, culminating in his rebellion regarding the Amalekites, triggered an expression of regret from the Lord. He told Samuel, "It repenteth me that I have set up Saul to be king: for he is turned back from following me, and hath not performed my commandments" (1 Sam. 15:11).

Saul had spared the king of the Amalekites and the best of their livestock, even though the Lord had commanded him to destroy all of them. When Samuel went to confront Saul with his transgression, Saul demonstrated a level of arrogance that defies belief, boasting, "I have performed the commandment of the Lord" (v. 13). When asked about the live animals Samuel was hearing, Saul pointed to the people, claiming that they "spared the best of the sheep and of the oxen, to sacrifice unto the Lord thy God" (v. 15). In verse 21 Saul repeated his defense: "The people took of the spoil, sheep and oxen, the chief of the things which should have been utterly destroyed, to sacrifice unto the Lord thy God in Gilgal."

Proverbs 6:16 says, "These six things doth the Lord hate: yea, seven are an abomination unto him." The first item on God's list is "a proud look," and the second is "a lying tongue" (v. 17). So far Saul was batting a thousand. Saul's pride and dishonesty did nothing to procure favor from the Lord, and the Lord restated his intention to remove him from power. That promise is what motivated Saul to confess his sin.

CONFESSION OR REPENTANCE

> Saul said unto Samuel, I have sinned: for I have transgressed the commandment of the Lord, and thy words: because I feared the people, and obeyed their voice. Now therefore, I pray thee, pardon my sin, and turn again with me, that I may worship the Lord. (1 Sam. 15:24–25)

In the late 1980s I dealt with a couple in the church where I ministered who were engaged in a lengthy impure relationship. The young man was single. The woman was somewhat older and married. Both had been Christians for some time and were well aware of the shame associated with their sin.

When confronted with his sin, the young man began to weep uncontrollably, confessing his sin and acknowledging his shame. His only concern was getting right with the Lord, and he was willing to take whatever steps necessary to accomplish that goal.

The woman's reaction, however, was different. While she acknowledged the relationship, there were no tears. Instead, she began to ask questions: "How many people know?" and "Can I deal with this without acknowledging my sin publicly?" She confessed her sin, but she didn't repent. She was more concerned about protecting her reputation than she was about reconciling with her God.

That is exactly what Saul did. Though he confessed with his lips, there was no obvious repentance. Repentance begins in the heart and demonstrates itself in obvious ways. Saul used several very common tactics to feign contrition for his sin.

1. He *qualified* his sin. First Samuel 15:20 states, "Saul said unto Samuel, Yea, I have obeyed the voice of the Lord." Then in verse 21 Saul said, "But the people . . . " Saul was unwilling to take personal responsibility for Israel's failure to obey the command of the Lord, blaming instead the people of Israel. Yet it was not the people who kept Agag, king of Amalek, alive to display as a trophy of their victory.

2. He *justified* his sin. Saul also made a special effort to explain *why* "the people" did what they did (v. 21). They disobeyed so that they would be better prepared to worship their God. They spared only the best of the animals, and they would be used for future sacrifices. Only a man whose thinking was very twisted would come to the insane conclusion that disobedience could somehow enhance worship.

3. He *minimized* his sin. When Saul finally acknowledged his sin—he did so only after Samuel reminded him that because of his sin God had rejected him as king—he once again qualified his sin, saying that he feared the people and *obeyed them rather than God* (1 Sam. 15:24). He then took it a step further, suggesting in verse 25 that Samuel could simply "pardon" his sin and they could go back and worship as if nothing had happened.

What occurred next is a vivid illustration of the consequences of Saul's disobedience. Samuel refused to return with Saul, and as he turned to leave, Saul grabbed Samuel's mantle and it ripped. "And Samuel said unto him, The Lord hath rent the kingdom of Israel from thee this day, and hath given it to a neighbour of thine, that is better than thou" (v. 28). That "neighbour" was a young shepherd boy, forty years his junior. His name was David, and Saul was about to learn far more about him than he wanted to know.

DISCUSSION QUESTIONS

1. Saul and David both committed sins that were sufficient to warrant their removal from office. Yet Saul was removed, while David retained his throne. What made David different from Saul?
2. Saul became king because Israel demanded a king. What did that demand demonstrate regarding Israel's attitude toward God?
3. What qualified Saul to be king in the eyes of the people? How did God indicate to Samuel that the choice of David was to be handled differently?
4. What two sins formed the core of Saul's claim that he had "performed the commandment of the Lord" (1 Sam. 15:13)?
5. Genuine repentance requires more than simply saying "I'm sorry." Why did Saul's "confession" fall short?

CHAPTER 2

MUSIC FOR A SIN-SICK SOUL

STRANGE THINGS HAPPEN IN THE heart of a man who chooses to defy the living God. Joy is gone. Peace is gone. Hope is all but gone, and depression begins to take hold. He spends his time mourning wrong choices, wondering what, if anything, can be done to reverse dreaded, bitter consequences. His days become unproductive, and his attitude becomes hostile and unbearable.

Saul's disobedience cost him his throne, along with his royal legacy. Yet Saul lost something far more precious than those. First Samuel 16:14 says, "The Spirit of the Lord departed from Saul, and an evil spirit from the Lord troubled him." Saul lost the discretion, courage, wisdom, and confidence that were the marks of God's leadership in his life, and those qualities were replaced with fear, uncertainty, envy, and despair. He was being tormented by the realization that things had changed. For the first time as king of Israel, he felt alone and unsure of himself. He was grieving the loss of God's presence in his life.

THE DEPARTURE OF GOD'S SPIRIT

Our understanding of the doctrine of eternal security makes it very hard to understand how the Spirit of the Lord could have withdrawn from Saul. That could *never* happen to a New Testament believer. How, then did it happen to Saul? God's method of dealing with believers in the Old Testament was very specific. Today, when a person becomes a Christian, the Spirit of

God takes up residence in his heart. In the Old Testament, however, the Spirit of God lived not in man's heart but in the tabernacle. The mercy seat, located in the holy of holies, was where God met with man. It was carefully hidden behind the veil of the temple, and the high priest alone was allowed entrance once a year to offer a sacrifice to atone for the sins of the people (Heb. 9:7).

In those days God spoke to His people through His prophets, who relayed God's message to priests and kings. For an Old Testament saint to experience the presence of God's Spirit, as did Saul, was rare. David did and understood that he could lose it, praying earnestly in Psalm 51:11 that God would not remove His Holy Spirit from him. Samson knew God's presence, lost it, and was unaware that it was gone (Judg. 16:20).

There were a few others who experienced the presence of God's Spirit, usually to provide guidance for a specific message or battle, including Othniel (Judg. 3:9–10), Gideon (Judg. 6:34), Jephthah (Judg. 11:29), Jahaziel (2 Chron. 20:14), Isaiah (Isa. 61:1), Ezekiel (Ezek. 11:5), and Micah (Mic. 3:8). There is, however, no documentation of any Old Testament saint knowing the security of God's presence that is readily available to every individual who trusts Christ today. Hebrews 13:5 says, "Let your conversation be without covetousness; and be content with such things as ye have: for he hath said, I will never leave thee, nor forsake thee." Saul, however, had no such promise.

AN EVIL SPIRIT FROM THE LORD

It is a terrible thing to presume upon God's goodness. Saul had become so accustomed to the benefits of God's presence that he failed to appreciate them properly. Losing the influence of God's Spirit was difficult enough, but it did not end there. Saul soon became aware of the presence of another spirit, also from the Lord but having a different character entirely.

Our perception of God as good and gracious provides little room for evil to come from Him. To say that this "evil spirit" came from the Lord is, for us, uncomfortable. Yet that is exactly what 1 Samuel 16:14 says. We know that God does not originate evil—His character will not permit it. We also understand, however, that God deals with men according to *their* character. When Pharaoh hardened his heart against God, God hardened Pharaoh's heart (Ex. 8:15; 9:12). Likewise, when Saul rejected God, God rejected Saul. Each of those men suffered a similar anguish of spirit as a result of God's judgment (Ex. 12:29-32; 1 Sam. 16:14; 1 Kings 21:27-29).

God is not vindictive. He doesn't hurt people simply to watch them suffer. Every choice God makes has a sound basis that is somehow connected to His holiness, which is the cornerstone of His character—love and justice rest on either side. Since His holiness demands righteousness, sin is unacceptable. Because God is loving, He takes no pleasure in punishing sin, and because He is just, He cannot overlook it. *His holiness demands payment*! Therefore, Saul's suffering is simply the natural result of God fulfilling His character in response to Saul's choices.

HELP FROM AN UNEXPECTED SOURCE

Saul's malady was obvious to everyone associated with him. His servants saw his distress and immediately recognized the problem. Informing Saul that "an evil spirit from God" was troubling him (1 Sam. 16:15), they suggested that he would benefit from the ministry of a gifted musician, someone who was skilled on a harp. Saul, desperate for relief from any source, commanded his servants to find such a man.

They didn't have to spend much time looking. One of Saul's servants had already spotted a man that would fit the bill nicely—"a son of Jesse the Bethlehemite, that is cunning in playing, and a mighty valiant man, and a man of war, and prudent in matters, and a comely person" (v. 18). This young man had one other character trait that qualified him for the job, one that Saul now lacked—the Lord was with him.

David, the anointed king of Israel, was in a field outside Bethlehem doing what he had done every day for many years—tending his family's sheep—when he was summoned for the second time to a meeting of great importance, this time at the king's residence in Gibeah. He must have been shocked to learn that he had been chosen to play his harp for the king. Thus far, it was only the sheep that had enjoyed his concerts. Keep in mind that he already knew that one day he would assume the throne currently occupied by the man for whom he was going to play. The irony is that Saul had no idea of God's orchestration of these events.

Everything that Saul was losing, David was gaining. Saul had lost God's presence; the Lord was now with David. Saul had lost his confidence; David's confidence had grown. Saul had lost his courage; David's courage had increased. Saul was losing his throne; David would soon occupy that chair. David was God's choice, a man after His own heart. God was preparing him to become king of Israel, and Saul was totally unaware of what was happening. Later, Saul would come to despise David and, in a fit of jealousy and rage, seek to take his life. Saul's first impression of David, however, was positive. It may have been his musical abilities, or it may have been the godly character qualities that David possessed that moved Saul's heart to embrace him. Most likely it was that David's appearance and attitude reminded him what it was like to enjoy the influence of God's Spirit. Whatever it was had a huge impact on Saul's opinion of the man who was chosen to replace him, because the Scripture says that Saul "loved him greatly" (v. 21).

THE SOOTHING IMPACT OF GODLY MUSIC

> It came to pass, when the evil spirit from God was upon Saul, that David took an harp, and played with his hand: so Saul was refreshed, and was well, and the evil spirit departed from him. (1 Sam. 16:23)

We are not told how long or how often David played for Saul, but we do know that his playing was effective. When David played, Saul was "refreshed." The music did its work, reviving Saul's spirit.

Music is a spiritual language that has the power to affect an individual's mood and alter a person's perspective. It can calm fears, encourage confidence, focus thinking, and restore peace. F. B. Meyer described the effect of David's music on Saul as follows:

> With David . . . the harp was the symbol of a soul at rest in God. All things were, therefore, his; all spoke to his soul of the harmonies subsisting in the unseen and eternal world. And it was because his own spirit was so perfectly harmonious with the nature of God and with the universe that he could cast the spell of calming and quieting influence over another.[3]

Music, when offered as a sacrifice of praise to God, also provides a spiritual benefit to believers, and David's ministry of music went far beyond playing the harp.

David was the author of half the psalms, many of which were written during times of great testing or distress. These "poems set to music" are repositories of great spiritual truth, usually reinforcing some foundational doctrine. Many of them are prayers offered in thanksgiving to God for His consistent character in caring for His people. Others document passionate petitions for God's mercy and forgiveness. Still others give us the sacred privilege of observing the heart of a yielded saint as he worships his God. As Matthew Henry wrote, "Every psalm either points directly to Christ, in his person, his character, and offices; or may lead the believer's thoughts to him. And the psalms are the language of the believer's heart, whether mourning for sin, thirsting after God, or rejoicing in him."[4]

Saul benefited from David's music, and that was the reason Saul summoned him to play. We must remember, however, that God does not reason as man, and what man plans for his own purpose is often designed to accomplish something entirely different in the purpose of God. From God's perspective, David's presence in Gibeah had a much broader meaning. God was beginning the process of transferring the throne. David was there to meet the king.

DISCUSSION QUESTIONS

1. When Saul rejected the word of the Lord, God rejected Saul as king. How did that rejection affect Saul's spirit? What was his greatest loss?
2. New Testament believers have absolute assurance of the abiding presence of the Holy Spirit. Many Old Testament saints knew the presence of God's Spirit as well. How was their experience different?
3. Scripture tells us that Saul experienced the influence of an "evil spirit from the Lord" (1 Sam. 16:14). We know that God is pure and holy and that evil could never originate with Him. What was the nature of the evil spirit?
4. Why was David's music effective in soothing Saul's spirit?
5. Saul summoned David to play for him because David's music calmed his depressed spirit. How did God use those encounters to accomplish His will in David's life?

CHAPTER 3

STANDING TALL IN THE SHADOW OF A GIANT

HE WAS A GIANT OF a man, this champion of the Philistine army. He measured in at nine feet, nine inches tall. His head, chest, and legs were protected by armor made of brass. His coat of mail weighed 125 pounds; the head of his spear fifteen pounds. He had a sword at his side and was preceded by an armor-bearer carrying a shield. A complete description is found in 1 Samuel 17:4–7.

How does a normal human do battle against such a foe? That was the question of the day, and the Israelite army had no answer. Even King Saul, a mighty man of valor who stood head and shoulders above any other man in Israel (1 Sam. 9:2), was unwilling to face this formidable enemy.

Goliath and the Philistine army were encamped on the west side of the valley of Elah; the Israelites on the east side. Every day for forty days, Goliath came forward to challenge the Israelite army (1 Sam. 17:16). He proposed that rather than engage in a full-scale war, their conflicts could be settled quickly and in a very simple way. He would fight the most skilled Israelite warrior. If he won, Israel would serve the Philistines. If the Israelite soldier won the battle, the Philistines would serve Israel (vv. 8–9).

Under normal circumstances such a proposal might be more than reasonable. But these were not normal circumstances. Goliath's defiance was not just a challenge that targeted Israel's fighting capabilities—it was a scornful challenge to their faith. The Spirit of God had departed from Saul, their king, and he was no longer sure of his ability or God's help. Unbelief destroys courage and turns otherwise brave men into cowards. Goliath knew he had the upper hand. Israel was backed into a corner, and there was no Israelite soldier who felt capable or possessed sufficient courage to answer Goliath's challenge.

David, though he had become an official member of Saul's court, was not a full-time resident of Gibeah. He was available to minister to Saul when needed, but at other times he would return to fulfill his primary responsibility—tending his sheep. First Samuel 17:15 tells us that at this point David had "returned from Saul to feed his father's sheep at Bethlehem." There, while in solitude with his God, David received essential training and encouragement to equip him for his future work. God was preparing him for the next step on his royal career path.

Meanwhile, the Philistine giant continued his relentless defiance of the Israelite army. When he first stated his challenge, he *came down* to stand in the valley, calling for an Israelite champion to come and meet him there (v. 8). Later, when it became apparent that there would be no response from Israel, he decided to approach them. Verse 23 says, "As he talked with them, behold, there came up the champion, the Philistine of Gath, Goliath by name, out of the armies of the Philistines, and spake according to the same words." He was *coming up* the slope on Israel's side of the valley—and fear drove the army of Israel to scatter (v. 24).

The last part of verse 23 says that David heard the challenge of the Philistine champion. David had arrived, humanly speaking, because of an errand he was assigned by his father. The task was simple:

> Take now for thy brethren an ephah of this parched corn, and these ten loaves, and run to the camp of thy brethren; And carry these ten cheeses unto the captain of their thousand, and look how thy brethren fare, and take their pledge. (vv. 17–18)

David found his brothers with the rest of Israel's army, in panic mode, immobilized by the threat of the enemy. He was talking with his brothers when he heard for the first time the voice that created Israel's panic.

COURAGE AMONG COWARDS

What David heard was offensive. This arrogant, overconfident, uncircumcised Philistine was publicly defying—mocking—the armies of the living God. But what David saw was embarrassing. The Israelite soldiers were retreating, and Goliath was making his way up the hill to confront them. Reading David's response, we might logically conclude that he never actually *saw* Goliath—surely he only *heard* the Philistine's challenge. No one who had actually seen him would have questioned the retreat. To David, however, size and strength were not the primary concerns. This pagan giant was ridiculing Israel's faith and laughing at their God! His God! Someone needed to respond, and if no one else was going to, he would.

David began by asking a question regarding the rumor that a reward was available for any man who could kill Goliath (v. 25). But the question David asked was almost as offensive as the giant's threats.

> What shall be done to the man that killeth this Philistine, and taketh away the reproach from Israel? for who is this uncircumcised Philistine, that he should defy the armies of the living God? (v. 26)

There was an element of disbelief in David's question. First, David could not believe that Goliath could be so bold as to mock the living God. More importantly, David could not believe that Goliath's challenge had not been answered.

David's older brother Eliab was one of those who took offense. He attacked his younger brother, accusing him of thinking too highly of himself and implying that his motives were less than pure: "Eliab sought for the splinter in his brother's eye, and was not aware of the beam in his own. The very things with which he charged his brother—presumption and wickedness of heart—were most apparent in his scornful reproof."[5] David, however, was not to be discouraged. His reply, though brief, was measured and to the point: "What have I now done? Is there not a cause?" (v. 29). This was no emotional, defensive outburst. David was intentionally dismissing the condescending attack of his brother and turning the focus back where it needed to be—on the challenge before them.

Words are potent, and David's words had a powerful impact. They made the rounds in the camp and were soon repeated to the king, who sent for David.

David's conversation with Saul (1 Sam. 17:32–37) was a contrast of emotions. David's assertions were filled with courage and confidence. Saul's words communicated fear and skepticism. In fact, David's first statement to Saul was intended to dispel the widespread fear of the Israelite army.

> Let no man's heart fail because of him; thy servant will go and fight with this Philistine. (v. 32)

Saul, however, was not convinced. He questioned David's ability, wisdom, and skill as a warrior, reminding him that his opponent was a "man of war from his youth" (v. 33).

What followed was an impressive report of David's improbable victories—killing a lion and a bear in defense of his flock. Faith overcomes fear and builds confidence, turning otherwise vulnerable men into heroes. It is apparent that these victories, wrought in the solitude of days spent tending sheep, were known only to David and his God. Yet those same victories, won in secret, provided David with enormous spiritual resources from which to draw when facing the biggest opponent of all. David's trust in the Lord made Goliath's boasting look foolish. In David's eyes, he was nothing more than an overgrown braggart, heaping to himself the wrath of a holy God, and David was God's choice to deliver judgment.

A SLING, A STONE, AND A SWORD

Learning of David's victories in the sheepfold must have given Saul confidence in his potential as a warrior because he agreed to let him go and offered his blessing, saying to him, "Go, and the Lord be with thee" (v. 37). It is also entirely possible that Saul was greatly relieved that someone had finally volunteered to face the giant. Whichever the case, Saul was going to do all that he could to assure a victory for his young warrior.

Saul's approach to fighting was much like that of Goliath. Size, strength, and skill were the primary concerns. Little advantage was gained by strategy. The goal was to overpower the opponent, and the bigger, stronger warrior, with rare exception, came out victorious. It is only reasonable, therefore, that Saul would offer David his armor (v. 38).

David, however, knew that his protection came not from shields and helmets crafted of brass. He understood that a faithful shepherd boy trusting in his God would have far more protection than a valiant king clad head to toe in the finest armor available. Having rejected Saul's offer, David gathered the tools of his trade, which included a shepherd's staff, a bag into which he placed five smooth stones that he collected from the brook in the valley, and his familiar sling (vv. 39–40). These weapons, though simple and small, provided all the firepower necessary to defeat the Philistine champion. Judges 20:16 says that among the children of Benjamin "there were seven hundred chosen men lefthanded; every one could sling stones at an hair breadth, and not miss." It is very likely that David possessed such skill with a sling. Having thus prepared, David "drew near to the Philistine" (1 Sam. 17:40).

Arrogance alters a man's thinking, causing him to consider caution unnecessary. When Goliath saw David, "he disdained him" (v. 42). That is, he dismissed David as an unworthy opponent and clearly expressed his disgust for all to hear:

> Am I a dog, that thou comest to me with staves? . . . Come to me, and I will give thy flesh unto the fowls of the air, and to the beasts of the field. (vv. 43–44)

David's battle plan was simple: don't be intimidated, yield your abilities to God, and trust Him for the victory.

No one anticipated a fair fight. Not Goliath. Not David's brothers. Not the Philistine or the Israelite armies. Not Saul, the man who sent David into the battle. They all would have agreed with Goliath that David was overmatched and unable, under any conceivable circumstances, to overcome such incredible odds. David would have agreed with that sentiment as well. David, however, was not the one fighting the battle. He was simply the instrument God had chosen to use, and in the end, Goliath was no match for Israel's God.

THE COURAGE OF A GODLY HEART

One of the key components of David's victory was courage. Without it, he would have been just as helpless as Saul, his brothers, and the entire army of Israel. With it, he was able to overcome impossible odds to prevail against an unstoppable foe, using absolutely ridiculous weapons. For a believer, courage is the consequence of a heart fully controlled by God. It is available only to those who are willing to embrace and exercise five spiritual concepts clearly seen in David's battle with the giant. They were conceived in his heart and manifested in his behavior.

1. Conviction—1 Samuel 17:29
   David heard the challenge and felt an obligation. The giant's blasphemous rant was offensive, as was the unresponsive Israelite army. David was motivated by a passion for his God and a sense of personal

responsibility. Conviction says that scriptural principles are more important than personal comfort. Is there a price to pay? Often there is, but conviction justifies the cost, placing appropriate value on priceless treasures.

2. Commitment—1 Samuel 17:32

David saw the opponent and was determined to face him. Courage is not the absence of fear. It is the strength to move forward in spite of it. David had to conquer his fear before he could defeat Goliath. Genuine victory comes only when we are committed to the battle without concern for likely personal sacrifice.

3. Confidence—1 Samuel 17:34-37

David measured the enemy and believed he could defeat him. There is no question that Goliath was an intimidating warrior, and David did not possess the size, strength, or skill to defeat him on his own. Yet David's confidence never wavered because he was trusting his God to produce the victory. He understood that "the weapons of our warfare are not carnal, but mighty through God to the pulling down of strong holds" (2 Cor. 10:4). Bears and lions posed little threat when God was fighting on David's behalf, and this Philistine giant would be as one of them. Conversely, battles fought by fleshly means never achieve spiritual victories.

4. Caution—1 Samuel 17:38-40

David noted the danger and prepared appropriately. Jesus told His disciples that they were to be "wise as serpents, and harmless as doves" (Matt. 10:16). Trusting God for victory does not preclude exercising caution in preparation. David rejected weapons offered by Saul because he had not "proved them" (1 Sam. 17:39). He was not familiar with them, nor were they appropriate for his fighting abilities. While God's blessing is not dependent on our abilities, it is subject to our willingness to use those abilities to honor Him.

5. Confrontation—1 Samuel 17:45–47

    David assessed the situation and moved forward by faith. Having identified his cause, expressed a willingness to make whatever sacrifice necessary, determined that the battle was his because the Lord would fight on his behalf, and properly armed himself for the battle, David had only one thing left to do—confront the enemy. At that point the battle was over. Goliath died when David removed his head, but he became a dead man the moment David yielded the battle to the Lord.

Every believer can identify with David's battle. Giants arise on every side, causing immeasurable discouragement and despair, destroying joy and making life miserable. God never intended it to be that way, and it doesn't have to be. Victory is readily available to those who are willing to acknowledge that "the battle is the Lord's" (v. 47).

DISCUSSION QUESTIONS

1. What was David's primary objection to Goliath's challenge?
2. Why was David's brother so offended by his younger brother's concern? What motivated his attack on David? What was David's response?
3. When King Saul heard of David's protests concerning the inactivity of Israel's army, he sent for him. What was Saul's initial reaction to David's offer to fight the giant? How was David's response to Goliath's challenge different from Saul's?
4. Why did David refuse Saul's offer to help him?
5. Goliath was obviously surprised when David appeared to confront him. What was Goliath's initial reaction when he saw his opponent? How did Goliath's response influence his approach to the battle?
6. What is courage? How is it developed?

CHAPTER 4

WINNING SPIRITUAL BATTLES AND LOSING GROUND

DAVID'S VICTORY OVER GOLIATH SET in motion a series of events that would shape his character and dramatically change his life. No longer was he just a poor shepherd boy from Bethlehem whose primary role was playing the harp for the king. People had taken notice of his courage, boldness, and skill as a warrior. He was now esteemed as a hero—the man who delivered the people of Israel from the tyranny of the Philistines—and there were certain benefits that naturally accompanied such a position. Saul had detailed a number of rewards that he would give the man who killed Goliath: "The king will enrich him with great riches, and will give him his daughter, and make his father's house free in Israel" (1 Sam. 17:25).

If David understood the acclaim he was receiving and expected special treatment as a result of it, he didn't show it. His responsibilities changed, but his behavior remained consistent with his character:

> David went out whithersoever Saul sent him, and behaved himself wisely: and Saul set him over the men of war, and he was accepted in the sight of all the people, and also in the sight of Saul's servants. (1 Sam. 18:5)

Saul loved him, the soldiers loved him, the people loved him, and the servants loved him. David's priority, however, remained the same—he was totally committed to serving and honoring the reigning king of Israel.

THE COMPASSIONATE FRIENDSHIP OF JONATHAN

Saul's immediate reaction to David's victory appears to be, at the very least, confusing. It seems on the surface that the king did not know David. How is it possible that King Saul, who had been comforted on so many occasions by the soft melody of David's harp and who had personally counseled David before sending him into battle against Goliath, did not know who David was? Yet 1 Samuel 17:55–58 relates that Saul requested that information not once but twice. The uncertainty pertained to David's family. Saul knew who David was, but he was unacquainted with his father, and Saul needed that information to guarantee that David's family received the benefits to which they were entitled.

Standing in the shadows, listening to the conversation, was Saul's son Jonathan, who had served in Israel's army for some time and was already an accomplished warrior. He commanded a third of Saul's troops and was well respected for his military expertise (1 Sam. 13:2–4). He, along with his father, would have been keenly impressed with David's courage and ability, and Jonathan was drawn to him immediately. It is said that there is nothing in the civilian world that can approach the bonding that occurs between soldiers in the war room, barracks, or foxhole. Lifelong friendships characterized by love and sacrifice are common. Jonathan and David established such a friendship.

We are not told how long it was before Jonathan learned that David had already been anointed as the next king of Israel. It appears that David shared that information immediately. One of the first things Jonathan did was to give David his robe and his sword, acknowledging his friendship and signifying his loyalty (1 Sam. 18:4). So strong was Jonathan's allegiance to David that their friendship survived the revelation of David's anointing as well as numerous attempts by his father to slay David.

First Samuel 20:14-17 reveals the details of a covenant between Jonathan and David. David's pledge, which extended to Jonathan's entire household, required him to show kindness to his family forever. Jonathan had already promised to give his life, if necessary, to protect David.

Loyalty requires sacrifice and a commitment to live for the prosperity of another. In some situations, that commitment can be costly. Jonathan encountered conflicting loyalties as he faced the reality that his father's attitude toward David had changed. Instead of embracing David as a friend and loyal subject, Saul now viewed David as his enemy, a traitor, and a serious threat to his throne.

THE COMPULSIVE FOOLISHNESS OF SAUL

At some point Jonathan may have told his father that David was the man chosen by God to replace him as king of Israel and that he had already been anointed by the prophet Samuel. Jonathan, however, was Saul's eldest son and the rightful heir to the throne. Saul would use whatever means necessary to see that his son occupied it, even if it meant killing God's anointed.

Because he trusted David, Saul had "set him over the men of war" (1 Sam. 18:5), and David was leading them into battle. Time after time, battle after battle, the Israelite army returned victorious. Celebrations had begun after the slaughter of Goliath, and the women came out to meet King Saul, singing, "Saul hath slain his thousands, and David his ten thousands" (v. 7).

Shakespeare famously wrote, "O, beware, my lord, of jealousy! / It is the green-eyed monster which doth mock / The meat it feeds on."[6] Jealousy feeds on itself and destroys the individual who tolerates it. Saul was already battling the distress of an evil spirit. He then fed his anger by brooding over what he imagined people were thinking.

> Saul was very wroth, and the saying displeased him; and he said, They have ascribed unto David ten thousands, and to me they have ascribed but thousands: and what can he have more but the kingdom? (v. 8)

Saul ignored the fact that David was fighting on his behalf and in his place. He dismissed the obvious loyalty that David displayed toward him, and it did not matter that David would have willingly laid down his life for him. Saul, in his warped thinking, disregarded the truth in order to feed his paranoia. The result of Saul's confused reasoning was unfounded suspicion. Verse nine says, "Saul eyed David from that day and forward." He assumed everything David did, good or bad, had evil intent.

So severe was Saul's distrust of David that he could no longer benefit from David's soothing music. He was unable to focus on the music because of his obsession with David's success. Someone once said, "Thoughts are actions in an incubator." As Saul contemplated his problem, an idea began to take shape in his mind. To put an end to any possibility that David would replace him as king of Israel, Saul decided to "smite David even to the wall" with his javelin (v. 11). Impulsive decisions are always unwise. In Saul's case, it was ineffective as well. The Scripture tells us that David "avoided out of his presence twice" (v. 11).

Remarkably, Saul's jealousy manifested itself in another, more significant way. He was obviously jealous of David's popularity, but the more serious problem was that David had the one thing Saul most regretted having lost—the presence of the Lord (v. 12). As a result, Saul was afraid of David. So he devised another, shrewder tactic to get rid of him, one that would not require his participation. He would encourage the Philistines to do the job for him—on the battlefield.

Though Saul would have thought his plan to be especially ingenious, most people with a minimal sense of morality would have called it evil. The scheme revealed in verses twenty to twenty-five was especially repulsive. He offered his daughter Michal in marriage to David in exchange for the lives of one hundred Philistines. Saul's plan was twofold. First, he was hoping that Michal would trip David up, perhaps causing him to lose his focus. Second, he intended for David to fall by the sword of the Philistines. What happened only increased Saul's fear. It turned out that Michal actually loved David, and David, with the Lord's help, was more than equal to the challenge he received from the king. He returned from the battle with evidence of two hundred Philistines slain, twice the number Saul requested. Saul's despair was growing, and he had no solution.

The one enduring character trait exhibited in Saul's life was persistence. He was firmly convinced that David was his enemy and determined to find a way to destroy him. In 1 Samuel 19 we read of three additional attempts made by Saul to kill David, all of which came to naught.

- He first gave all his servants (including his son Jonathan) a direct order to kill David (v. 1). Jonathan's immediate response was to inform David of his father's intentions and encourage him to hide. He then returned to his father and reasoned with him, eventually convincing him to rescind the order. When Jonathan advised David of the favorable report, David returned to Saul.
- Saul's kindness, however, was short lived. Having learned of David's latest success in battle against the Philistines, Saul again found himself brooding bitterly over David's popularity. For a third time, Saul tried to pierce David with his javelin while David sought to comfort him (vv. 8-10). And for the third time, David "slipped away out of Saul's presence" (v. 10).
- Saul then sent "messengers" (assassins) to David's house with an assignment to slay him the next morning (vv. 11-16). Michal, David's wife, learned of the trap, warned David, helped him escape, and devised a plan to mislead the intended assassins.

Saul was being driven by hatred, fueled by a false assumption that David was his enemy. Circumstances had influenced his thinking, and his imagination did the rest. Saul knew that the Lord had departed from him and was now helping David. He knew that the people were impressed with David's leadership and captivated by David's victories on the battlefield. Their celebrations, normally reserved for him, were now held in honor of David. He knew that his son Jonathan had become a close, faithful friend of David. He knew that his days as king were numbered and that David was God's chosen replacement. He also knew that there was nothing he could do to stop it. That thought drove Saul mad.

THE CONSISTENT FAITHFULNESS OF DAVID

It would be irresponsible to ignore David's attitude in all this. The Scripture takes great care to inform us that David "behaved himself wisely" (1 Sam. 18:5, 14, 30), and David's response is astonishing. Remember that Saul was obsessed with killing David, even though David had done nothing wrong. Yet there was no indication of anger in any of David's responses. Not once did he attempt to retaliate. He never uttered a word to criticize Saul. David was a loyal subject of the king, and David's faithful behavior only intensified Saul's wrath.

Tending sheep required a special kind of self-discipline. Days were long and hot, and nights were lonely and cold. The seclusion alone was often enough to create a sense of frustration in the heart of the most experienced shepherd. While there, David's relationship with God grew to become intensely personal, and his experiences taught him to trust the Lord no matter the size of the trial. David's character was shaped by those trials in the pasture. Lessons learned in the sheepfold served David well in Saul's court.

The first character trait that stands out in David's life is *dependability*. First Samuel 18:5 says that "David went out whithersoever Saul sent him, and behaved himself wisely." Were any of David's assignments unpleasant? Did he resent specific duties? If he did, it's not apparent from Scripture. Every reference to David's activities while serving Saul is positive. David did his best, even when doing so put him in danger. First Samuel 18:30 summarizes David's attitude and status: "David behaved himself more wisely than all the servants of Saul; so that his name was much set by."

David benefited greatly from his newly gained celebrity status. The people loved him, his influence soared, and though we are not told it is true, it is reasonable to assume that he gained some material prosperity as well. At the very least he was dressing better. Those things, however, were not a reflection of David's spirit. David, while tending his sheep, had learned well the importance of *sacrifice*. It is only through sacrifice that genuine value is revealed. David would have gladly given his life, if necessary, to fulfill his responsibilities.

The third character trait we notice is *humility*. In one of Saul's attempts to trap David, he sent his servants to David with a message:

> Behold, the king hath delight in thee, and all his servants love thee: now therefore be the king's son in law. (v. 22)

Surely David would have been anticipating such a visit. After all, one of the rewards for killing Goliath was the hand of Saul's daughter in marriage. David's answer is found in the next verse: "Seemeth it to you a light thing to be a king's son in law, seeing that I am a poor man, and lightly esteemed?" Surely there was a misunderstanding. David could no longer be called "poor," and how could he interpret his status as "lightly esteemed"? His response was an indication of his character. Though his station in life had changed, his humility persevered.

Finally, David's character was demonstrated by his *kindness*. There was in David's heart no spirit of vengeance, no bitterness over his tribulations, and no sense of hatred for his pursuer. Never did he seek to retaliate. Later, when the opportunity to assassinate the king presented itself to David at the cave in the wilderness of Engedi, he responded with unthinkable mercy (1 Sam. 24:1–5). Saul was pursuing David to kill him. Yet David refused to harm the king. First Samuel 24:6 records David's answer to his men when they encouraged him to take advantage of Saul's vulnerability:

> The LORD forbid that I should do this thing unto my master, the Lord's anointed, to stretch forth mine hand against him, seeing he is the anointed of the Lord.

David knew that his protection came from the Lord and that in God's timing he would replace Saul as king of Israel.

David's life was challenging. He ministered to Saul with his harp and Saul repaid him with an attempt on his life. He commanded Saul's army, always slaying the Philistines "with a great slaughter" (1 Sam. 19:8; 23:5) and securing Israel's freedom, and Saul rewarded him with traps and schemes designed to end his life. David was committed to serving Saul. Yet Saul was obsessed with killing David.

Psalm 59 was penned during this time. There we find an indication of the spiritual battles David was facing. He called those who were seeking his life "workers of iniquity," pleading that God would save him from "bloody men" (v. 2). He protested that he was being hunted unjustly—"Lo, they lie in wait for my soul: the mighty are gathered against me; not for my transgression, nor for my sin, O Lord" (v. 3)—and he cried out for God's deliverance: "Deliver me from mine enemies, O my God: defend me from them that rise up against me" (v. 1).

The psalm concludes with David declaring the source of his confidence:

> But I will sing of thy power; yea, I will sing aloud of thy mercy in the morning: for thou hast been my defence and refuge in the day of my trouble. Unto thee, O my strength, will I sing: for God is my defence, and the God of my mercy. (vv. 16–17)

David fully embraced the principle found in Romans 12:19: "Vengeance is mine; I will repay, saith the Lord." His composure during this time of testing is a reflection of that belief. God was his defense; He would execute vengeance on those who were guilty. David would simply trust his God and continue to "[behave] himself wisely in all his ways" (1 Sam. 18:14).

DISCUSSION QUESTIONS

1. At the end of 1 Samuel 17, King Saul asked a puzzling question: "Whose son is this youth?" (v. 55). How is it possible that Saul was unacquainted with David's family?
2. After David's victory in the battle with Goliath, he received additional responsibility, which included leadership in Israel's army. As David's victories began to mount, Saul's attitude toward him began to change. What was the motivation for Saul's change of opinion concerning David? In what ways did Saul change how he treated David?
3. David's response to Saul's aggression demonstrated wisdom beyond his years. What character qualities did David demonstrate as he dealt with the erratic behavior of his king?
4. Because of the challenges that Saul was facing, David never knew what to expect. How was David able to maintain his composure and concentrate on fulfilling his responsibilities?

CHAPTER 5
THE FUGITIVE KING

JONATHAN KNEW HIS FATHER WELL. He was Saul's eldest son, the official heir to the throne, and he had been the senior commander of his father's army. Therefore, he enjoyed exclusive access to Saul's thinking and plans. Jonathan was convinced that his father would do nothing, "either great or small," without telling him (1 Sam. 20:2). That wealth of vital information was one of the great benefits of David's friendship with Jonathan.

When David returned from Naioth, where he had gone to escape from Saul's would-be assassins, he went immediately to see his friend Jonathan (v. 1). He was concerned about the king's aggressive attitude toward him. Though he was unable to determine the reason for Saul's attacks or gain a clear understanding of his crime, he was sure that death was but a step away. Jonathan's immediate reaction was to assure David that his worries were unfounded. Yet when Jonathan next talked with his father, he learned that David's fears were indeed accurate. The arrows flew (a predetermined signal established to communicate to David Saul's continued hostility), and David fled (vv. 35–42).

LIVING IN EXILE

David's departure began a period of what was likely about ten years that he lived in exile. His primary goal in leaving was to escape the vicious attacks of Saul. But fleeing meant that other relationships would be interrupted as well, relationships to which David's departure brought great sadness rather than joy. He had to leave Samuel, his trusted counselor, the one who had anointed him as king. He would never see Samuel again. He had to leave his wife, Michal, who loved, warned, and protected him at her own peril. He also had to leave his friend Jonathan. The tenderness of their parting demonstrated a sincere friendship that would not soon be forgotten. Vows were recalled and blessings offered as David began his flight.

Relationships are precious. They form the core of our social existence and help sustain us in times of challenge. Losing them hurts.

David's first stop was in Nob to see Ahimelech the priest. Two things were accomplished during this visit. First, he obtained bread for him and his men (1 Sam. 21:3–6). Second, David procured a sword while there, and what a sword it was. Ahimelech offered him the only sword available.

> The sword of Goliath the Philistine, whom thou slewest in the valley of Elah, behold, it is here wrapped in a cloth behind the ephod: if thou wilt take that, take it: for there is no other save that here. And David said, There is none like that; give it me. (v. 9)

David's departure from Nob was hastened by the presence of one of Saul's servants, whom David recognized, a man named Doeg, who would surely inform Saul of his whereabouts (v. 7). David's retreat meant that he escaped the wrath of Saul, but David's benefactor did not fare so well. When Saul heard Doeg's report, he declared Ahimelech and all the priests of Nob guilty of treason and sentenced them to death. Doeg was appointed as executioner and eighty-five priests and the entire city of Nob were slain (1 Sam. 22:6–19).

Meanwhile, David's flight took him to a place twenty-three miles from Nob that no one would expect him to visit, especially when he was fleeing from the king of Israel. Apparently, David had a temporary lapse in his wise behavior, because he paid a visit to Gath, the Philistine home of Goliath

(1 Sam. 21:10–15). Perhaps he thought that he would be well received because he was Saul's enemy or that his victory over Goliath had faded from their memory. At any rate, it wasn't long until the king's servants began to recognize him. They knew who he was and were aware of his reputation in Israel. When David realized that he had been discovered, his wisdom returned and he pretended to be mad, changing his behavior, scratching the doors of the gate, and drooling on his beard. His plan worked—they judged him to be a fool and sent him on his way.

LIVING IN CAVES

After he left Gath, David took up residence in a cave at Adullam (1 Sam. 22:1–5). This was the first of two cave dwellings for David, the second being in the wilderness of Engedi.

Promises hold their value only as long as there is reason to believe that fulfillment remains possible. David must have had a difficult time with that assurance when he found himself living desolate, alone, and without hope in a dark, damp cave. Yet somehow he knew that the Lord had not forsaken him. David penned Psalm 142 while hiding in the cave at Adullam. The despair is palpable as we read David's words.

> I looked on my right hand, and beheld, but there was no man that would know me: refuge failed me; no man cared for my soul. I cried unto thee, O Lord: I said, Thou art my refuge and my portion in the land of the living. Attend unto my cry; for I am brought very low: deliver me from my persecutors; for they are stronger than I. Bring my soul out of prison, that I may praise thy name: the righteous shall compass me about; for thou shalt deal bountifully with me. (vv. 4–7)

Because Adullam was in Judah and close to his home in Bethlehem, news of David's whereabouts spread quickly. Soon David found himself surrounded by four hundred men, all of whom were in distress and sorely displeased with

Saul's leadership. This assembly of men, which later grew to six hundred (1 Sam. 23:13), formed the core of David's military battalion.

Among those who joined David were the members of his own family, including his father and mother, whom he took to Mizpeh in Moab, the home of David's great-grandmother Ruth. There he secured the king's promise to protect his parents. Then David returned to his men waiting in the hold at Adullam.

Advice from the prophet Gad led David back to the land of Judah—to the forest of Hareth. While there, David learned of an attack by the Philistines on Keilah, a walled city just to the west of his campsite (vv. 1–5). David's first instinct was to go and defend the city. He had been running and hiding for some time. Now he had a band of men who could fight, and a battle would, at the very least, raise his spirits. He would be accomplishing something positive if he could deliver Keilah from the Philistines. David's men, however, were not sure it was wise to confront the Philistines when they already had their hands full simply staying ahead of Saul. But after inquiring of the Lord twice, David and his men attacked the Philistines "and smote them with a great slaughter" (v. 5).

Saul, eager for any good news, was thrilled when he learned that David was in Keilah. Still self-deceived and confused, he somehow concluded that God had favored him:

> God hath delivered him into mine hand; for he is shut in, by entering into a town that hath gates and bars. (v. 7)

Saul gathered his men and began preparing to besiege David in Keilah.

David, however, had his own informers. When he learned of Saul's "secretly practiced mischief against him" (v. 9), he called Abiathar—the priestly son of Ahimelech who had caught up with David, having escaped the slaughter at Nob (1 Sam. 22:20)—to seek the Lord's guidance (1 Sam. 23:9–12). He wanted to know whether the men of Keilah, whom he had just delivered from the Philistines, would turn him over to Saul.

Fear exerts extraordinary influence. It begins by manipulating an individual's reasoning, ultimately changing his perception, motivation, and actions. The Lord revealed to David that these men of Keilah, though they had just been granted deliverance by the Lord at the hands of David and his men, were so driven by fear that they would not hesitate to deliver them up to Saul, and David and his men, who now numbered six hundred, wasted no time departing.

First Samuel 23:14–29 documents an uncertain period of time in David's exile. It could have been weeks, months, or even years that passed during this time. He traveled through the wilderness, from Ziph to Maon, always conscious of the relentless pursuit of Saul and his army. The events reported in this passage testify to the sovereign purpose and power of God as He protected the future king of Israel.

James 1:17 says that "every good gift and every perfect gift is from above, and cometh down from the Father of lights, with whom is no variableness, neither shadow of turning." Yet all believers endure times when the goodness of God is obscured by the circumstances of this life. David knew he was destined to become king of Israel, but his focus was not on the throne. Instead, he was trying desperately to evade the pursuit of Saul, a vicious man whose only desire was to kill him. David was in desperate need of a "good gift" from God.

He received it in the form of an unexpected visit from his devoted friend Jonathan.

> Jonathan Saul's son arose, and went to David into the wood, and strengthened his hand in God. (1 Sam. 23:16)

Jonathan not only knew that God had anointed David to be king, but he had also surrendered to God's will. He would serve under David's authority, in spite of his father's determination to prevent it. What neither of them knew was that this was the last time they would see each other. Jonathan would die in battle before David became king.

David's second cave experience occurred in the mountains of Engedi. He was in the desert of Maon when Saul finally backed him into a corner, having learned of David's location from the Ziphites, who were far too eager to betray their own countryman and more than happy to assist in his capture (vv. 19-24). When David learned of Saul's pursuit, he hurried down the other side of the mountain. In the meantime, God in His sovereignty moved the Philistines to invade the land of Judah, and Saul's attention was temporarily redirected toward them (vv. 25-28). David took advantage of that opportunity to find refuge in the "strong holds at Engedi" (v. 29), a mountainous region six or seven hours from his campsite in the wilderness of Maon.

Saul returned from his battle with the Philistines to find that David had moved once again, so he took three thousand men with him to Engedi and continued his pursuit "upon the rocks of the wild goats" (1 Sam. 24:1-2). His all-consuming desire was to kill the man who threatened his throne, the man who had God's blessing on his life.

The events described in 1 Samuel 24:3-4 would seem too incredible to believe if it weren't for the fact that God was clearly at work. David and his men had found refuge in one of the numerous caves in the area when Saul wandered in alone. He was there to "cover his feet" (an Eastern euphemism for relieving himself, which explains why he was alone). Suddenly David found himself in a position to seize the throne immediately. All he had to do was take advantage of the opportunity God had given him.

> The men of David said unto him, Behold the day of which the Lord said unto thee, Behold, I will deliver thine enemy into thine hand, that thou mayest do to him as it shall seem good unto thee. Then David arose, and cut off the skirt of Saul's robe privily. (v. 4)

Notice how David's men chose to characterize their good fortune. In essence, they were saying, "This is clear evidence that God has given Saul into your hand. He has fulfilled His commitment to you." When God made such a promise is not disclosed, and there is no record of it in Scripture. That David had reservations about such an assumption is clear from what he did. He chose not to kill Saul. Instead, he quietly cut off a small piece of his robe, and even that made him feel guilty (v. 5).

David's men all had reasons to desire Saul's death. They were with David because of issues they had with Saul's oppressive leadership (1 Sam. 22:1–2), and it was a simple matter for them to justify their advice by claiming God provided the opportunity.

Here is an important scriptural principle: *knowing God's will requires more than simply having an opportunity to do what we want.* It is not unusual for believers to make serious mistakes regarding God's will because they lack discernment. Not every opportunity comes from God. Many years later, in the twilight of his reign, David had a similar opportunity to do something that he wanted to do. But 1 Chronicles 21:1 tells us that it was Satan who "provoked David to number Israel." On that occasion wisdom deserted David and he yielded to the temptation.

Saul left the cave as he came in, unaware of David's presence or actions. He had not been gone long, however, when he heard a voice calling him from behind.

> David also arose afterward, and went out of the cave, and cried after Saul, saying, My lord the king. And when Saul looked behind him, David stooped with his face to the earth, and bowed himself. (1 Sam. 24:8)

When Saul looked behind him to see who was calling, he did not see a warrior with a spear in his hand. Instead, he saw David, his presumed enemy, bowing before him and addressing him as "my lord the king."

David's comments to Saul display a sincerity and tenderness that can be explained only by godly character. You can almost hear the agony in David's voice as he sought to reason with the king he loved and longed to serve:

> Wherefore hearest thou men's words, saying, Behold, David seeketh thy hurt? Behold, this day thine eyes have seen how that the Lord had delivered thee to day into mine hand in the cave: and some bade me kill thee: but mine eye spared thee; and I said, I will not put forth mine hand against my lord; for he is the Lord's anointed. Moreover, my father, see, yea, see the skirt of thy robe in my hand: for in that I cut off the skirt of thy robe, and killed thee not, know thou and see that there is neither evil nor transgression in mine hand, and I have not sinned against thee; yet thou huntest my soul to take it. (vv. 9–11)

David wanted desperately to communicate one simple message to Saul: "I'm not your enemy!" In this short conversation, he referred to Saul as "my lord the king" (v. 8), "the Lord's anointed" (v. 10), and "my father" (v. 11)—all terms that conveyed his respect and affection—and he could not understand why Saul was so bitterly determined to destroy him.

Although David's restraint was a remarkable display of his strength of character, choosing to spare Saul was more than a conscious act of self-discipline. In Luke 6:45 Jesus said, "A good man out of the good treasure of his heart bringeth forth that which is good; and an evil man out of the evil treasure of his heart bringeth forth that which is evil: for of the abundance of the heart his mouth speaketh." By his actions David revealed his heart.

1. *David's Mercy*

    David's decision to spare Saul was abnormal, especially in the context of war. Had the circumstances been reversed, Saul would have eagerly taken David's life without the slightest hesitation or remorse, justifying his actions by declaring David to be his enemy. Yet Saul was not David's enemy, and the servant's earnest desire was to be reconciled to his king. Why would David seek the death of the one he loved and wanted to serve? Instead, David hoped that by showing mercy, he would be able to change Saul's attitude.

2. *David's Mission*

   David's destiny had already been decided. Samuel had anointed him to be the next king of Israel, and once Saul was removed, David would take the throne. In David's mind there was no uncertainty or apprehension about God's purpose or plan. Though Saul understood what God was doing as well, he was determined to prevent it. When David cut off the hem of Saul's robe, he was demonstrating in a symbolic way what God was doing. He would replace Saul as king. God had ordered it, and there was no way Saul could stop it from happening.

3. *David's Motive*

   In Psalm 32:2 David wrote, "Blessed is the man unto whom the Lord imputeth not iniquity, and in whose spirit there is no guile." In Psalm 34:13 he said, "Keep thy tongue from evil, and thy lips from speaking guile." In an older sense, guile is the process of using artful deception or shrewdness to achieve a particular goal. In a more general sense, its meaning can include dishonesty or duplicity. David demonstrated none of those qualities in his dealings with Saul. When he said in verse 11, "Know thou and see that there is neither evil nor transgression in mine hand, and I have not sinned against thee," he was assuring Saul that his words were true and his motives pure.

4. *David's Meekness*

   David's threat to Saul's throne, from a human perspective, was miniscule. David had six hundred disgruntled men. Saul had three thousand highly skilled warriors. Though David was by no means weak, he was very much overmatched. Verse 14 conveys David's opinion of the situation and poses some challenging questions for Saul to ponder: "After whom is the king of Israel come out? after whom dost thou pursue? after a dead dog, after a flea." David had no desire to resist—nor was he capable of resisting—the battlefield skills of Saul and Israel's army. That's why he was fleeing. Saul had no defensible reason to fear, suspect, or hunt David.

Chapter 24 ends with Saul confessing his sin and acknowledging that the things David said were true (vv. 16–21). In his response to David, "Saul described three possible levels of life: the divine level, where we return good for evil; the human level, where we return good for good and evil for evil; and the demonic level, where we return evil for good."[7] Saul conceded that David had treated him not as an enemy but as a friend and that he had returned evil for David's kindness.

Included in Saul's answer to David was a sincere though selfish request. Since David would eventually become king, Saul asked David to make a solemn promise to spare his family (v. 21). That concern had already been addressed in the covenant David made with Saul's son Jonathan, so David did not hesitate to agree (v. 22).

Saul's emotional response to David's words (verse 16 says that he "lifted up his voice, and wept") was simply an expression of temporary remorse that included no change in Saul's attitude or actions. Though David got a brief respite from Saul's pursuit, he was not free to stop running. Verse 22 says that "Saul went home." Even so, trusting Saul was not wise, and David was taking no chances. He took his men back into hiding.

Though David won many battles in his life, none was more significant than the battle in the cave at Engedi. No blows were exchanged, no one was killed, and no victory was publicly acknowledged. Yet David walked away with a quiet, unassuming assurance that he had done the right thing. God was in complete control of the circumstances of his life as well as the final destination. He would let God be the judge of his character and wait on Him to impose His will.

DISCUSSION QUESTIONS

1. David spent ten years avoiding Saul's angry pursuit. There are some who criticize David for fleeing, claiming that he experienced a lapse of faith. Yet Scripture never condemns David for running. Do you believe that David was acting within the boundaries of God's will when he escaped from Saul?
2. How does fear relate to faith in the life of a believer? Does God ever use fear in a positive way? How does caution differ from fear?
3. What was the difference, if any, between David's fear and that of the men of Keilah discussed in 1 Samuel 23:9–12?
4. In 1 Samuel 24 we learn that David had an opportunity to put an end to Saul's evil pursuit. David, however, refused to kill Saul because he was "the LORD's anointed" (v. 6). How did David use the opportunity as an attempt to repair his broken relationship with Saul?
5. What can we learn about David's heart from his decision to spare the king?
6. Believers often talk about God opening and closing doors as a means of knowing His will. Is an "open door" always an indication of God's approval?

CHAPTER 6

IN THE COMPANY OF FOOLS

CHAPTERS 25 AND 26 OF the book of 1 Samuel provide an interesting contrast between two sides of the same man. In the last chapter we learned about David's strength of character when facing the temptation to slay the anointed king of Israel, who was seeking to end his life. His discipline would not allow him to act impulsively. Yet when David was confronted in 1 Samuel 25 with the refusal of a wealthy though foolish shepherd to provide essential food and necessities for his men, his anger took over. Suddenly self-control was nowhere to be found.

Then in 1 Samuel 26 we learn the details of an experience that sounds strangely similar to the events of chapter 24. David once again refused to slay Saul when the opportunity presented itself. While there are some who insist that this account is simply an alternate presentation of the former event, they are not the same. In chapter 24 Saul entered David's presence unknowingly; in chapter 26 David intentionally invaded Saul's camp. The events in chapter 24 occurred during the day; in chapter 26 the encounter happened at night. The first encounter involved David cutting off a piece of Saul's robe; in the second he took Saul's spear and "cruse of water" (26:11). Though David was much bolder (he initiated the invasion of Saul's camp) in the second encounter, his wisdom again led him to avoid what would have been a tragic mistake. He refused to kill his king.

A FOOLISH SHEPHERD

Samuel had died (1 Samuel 25:1). As a result, "all the Israelites were gathered together, and lamented him." One commentary explains, "Since the days of Moses and Joshua, no man had arisen to whom the covenant nation owed so much as to Samuel, who has been justly called the reformer and restorer of the theocracy."[8] Israel's relationship with Samuel while he was alive was not always good, and they had rejected his warning against choosing a king (1 Sam. 8:4-19). At his death, however, the people honored him.

NABAL'S ARROGANCE

Rather than attending the funeral, David, knowing that Saul would have spies there and seeking to distance himself from Saul, took his men and traveled southward to the wilderness of Paran, a desert area near the mountains in the southern part of Judah. While there, David and his men encountered a team of shepherds employed by a man of substantial means named Nabal, for whom they provided protection. It was appropriate for them to show their appreciation by providing food and water for their benefactors. To refuse was more than an insult; it was an unsavory display of rudeness, demonstrating intentional disrespect. Yet when David sent messengers to Nabal requesting provisions for his men, Nabal did indeed refuse, with unbelievable arrogance:

> Nabal answered David's servants, and said, Who is David? and who is the son of Jesse? there be many servants now a days that break away every man from his master. Shall I then take my bread, and my water, and my flesh that I have killed for my shearers, and give it unto men, whom I know not whence they be? (1 Sam. 25:10-11)

Nabal's answer, though ugly and offensive, accurately reflected his character. Scripture describes him as being "churlish and evil" (v. 3). *Churlish* is an unfamiliar word that indicates a mean, insolent personality. One of

Nabal's servants, who knew him well, said of him, "He is such a son of Belial, that a man cannot speak to him" (v. 17). Nabal's wife agreed. Interceding with David on behalf of her husband, she said, "Let not my lord, I pray thee, regard this man of Belial, even Nabal: for as his name is, so is he; Nabal is his name, and folly is with him" (v. 25).

Nabal was a cruel man with a mean spirit. Nobody liked him, and he was impossible to deal with. His greatest problem, however, was that he was a fool (not simpleminded but without wisdom), and his foolish actions would ultimately lead to his death.

DAVID'S ANGER

Ingratitude is difficult to abide, and we are admonished in Scripture to respond without offense when we encounter such disrespect (Luke 6:28–29). Though anger should always be avoided, there are times when a measured, controlled response to unjustified contempt is warranted. David had responded with such restraint to the vile, disgusting defiance of Goliath.

David's reaction to Nabal's disrespect, however, went far beyond righteous indignation; it was intensely personal. He was irritated that Nabal would reward his kindness with evil (v. 21). He was incensed that his men were treated with such disrespect (1 Samuel 25:14 says that Nabal "railed on them"), and he was insulted that Nabal had characterized him as a worthless, rebellious vagrant (v. 10). David responded not with measured control but with enraged recklessness. He was determined to punish Nabal for his selfishness, and there was no reason to delay the judgment.

There was little doubt about David's intent. He gathered two-thirds of his army (four hundred men), armed them, and headed to Carmel to deal with Nabal. His plan was to kill not only Nabal but "all that pertain to him" (v. 22). David was following the dictates of his flesh, demanding that his selfish desire for vengeance be satisfied. What happened next stopped David in his tracks, brought him to his senses, and kept him from sinning against the Lord.

ABIGAIL'S ARBITRATION

> Keep back thy servant also from presumptuous sins; let them not have dominion over me: then shall I be upright, and I shall be innocent from the great transgression. (Ps. 19:13)

These words penned by David reveal the sensitivity of his heart to the possibility of impulsive sin. He knew what he was capable of and that he needed help overcoming his temptation. He made the petition for such a time as this, and God answered it. David was on his way to meet Nabal when he was intercepted by Abigail, Nabal's wife.

Abigail was "a woman of good understanding, and of a beautiful countenance" (1 Sam. 25:3). She also knew that her husband was less than honorable in his dealings. When one of Nabal's servants explained to her that her husband had dealt scornfully with those who had protected them, she quickly prepared a peace offering to counteract what she knew would be coming. Then she set off to meet with David before he reached her husband. Her approach and attitude helped defuse an explosive situation.

Her Respect—1 Samuel 25:18-24

It is apparent that Abigail was essential to her husband's success. Not only did she administer the household, but she also served as an able and persuasive negotiator for her husband. Knowing that David was on his way to even the score with Nabal, she hurriedly gathered the supplies that should have been provided originally. Then she sent her servants before her with the bounty. When she finally met David "by the covert on the hill" (v. 20), she got off of her donkey, fell on her face before him, and called him lord (vv. 23-24). Abigail had the foresight, wisdom, and humility to act with urgency while still trusting the Lord for deliverance, and she was willing to show appropriate respect to the next king of Israel.

Her Repentance—1 Samuel 25:25–31

Abigail had no part in her husband's wretched response to David and his men, yet she took full responsibility for the offense, acknowledging the poor judgment of her husband and seeking to make amends. She had spiritual discernment that her husband lacked. While her husband, who was a loyal supporter of King Saul, saw David as a rebel seeking to overthrow the throne, Abigail saw him as Saul's divinely appointed successor. How she knew is not disclosed, but Abigail's understanding of what was happening is astounding. She knew that David was acting out of a sincere desire to fulfill the will of God (v. 28). She knew that Saul's efforts to kill David were hopeless because God was protecting him (v. 29). She knew that David would soon occupy the throne of Israel (v. 30). She also understood that if David chose to carry out his plan to exact revenge on Nabal, the Lord would be displeased and David would live to regret it (v. 31). She saw David as a man whom God was using, a man whose heart was set to seek his God.

Her Request—1 Samuel 25:28, 31

Abigail asked for two things. First, she sought forgiveness (v. 28). Though she was not personally involved in the transgression, she felt a sense of guilt, as did Nabal's entire household.

Her second request pertained to her security after David became king. The petition is found in verse 31: "When the LORD shall have dealt well with my lord, then remember thine handmaid." Because of David's opinion of her husband, she was sure the years ahead would be challenging. If she could persuade David to remember her kind treatment of him during the current crisis, perhaps she could avoid the harsh conditions her husband was sure to face in the future.

Her Reward—1 Samuel 25:32-44

David's response to Abigail was motivated by sincere gratitude for Abigail's courage and wisdom but even more so for God's sovereign protection (vv. 32-33). God had often protected David from his enemies. In this case, God had protected David from himself, thus keeping him from doing something that would hinder his relationship with God and greatly harm his influence in Israel. After receiving the food and supplies she had brought, David assured Abigail of his support and then sent her on her way (v. 35).

Abigail went home to find her husband in a drunken stupor brought on by a night of partying (v. 36). Perhaps he was celebrating the way he had put David in his place by rejecting his request for help. Maybe he was rejoicing over the money made recently at the sheep market. The irony is that it was the protection of David's men that made the celebration possible. When he finally sobered up the next morning, Abigail told him what had happened, and the Scripture says that Nabal's "heart died within him, and he became as a stone" (v. 37). He was so overcome with anger, grief, and fear that he was unable to function normally. Did he have a heart attack or a stroke? Did he go mad? The Bible doesn't say. All we know is that ten days later he died—a clear consequence of God's judgment (v. 38).

When David heard the news, he first rejoiced in God's goodness (v. 39). God had kept him from sinning, and He had once again given him victory over an enemy.

David then asked Abigail to be his wife, and she agreed without hesitation (1 Sam. 25:39-42). It may seem a bit strange that Abigail accepted so quickly. There does not appear to be any sense of regret or sorrow on her part at Nabal's passing. Most likely what she felt was a sense of liberation. Nabal was a foolish man—a "man of Belial" (v. 25)—and no one would have suffered that burden more acutely than Abigail.

A FOOLISH KING

Saul's last statement to David, found in 1 Samuel 24, indicated sorrow over how he had treated David, gratitude for how David had treated him, and a clear understanding that God had chosen David to replace him as king of Israel. But whatever regret Saul felt was temporary. First Samuel 26 begins with Saul again pursuing David.

> The Ziphites came unto Saul to Gibeah, saying, Doth not David hide himself in the hill of Hachilah, which is before Jeshimon? Then Saul arose, and went down to the wilderness of Ziph, having three thousand chosen men of Israel with him, to seek David in the wilderness of Ziph. (vv. 1-2)

Once again, the Ziphites were responsible for betraying David's whereabouts to Saul. David, perhaps thinking that Saul's obsession with killing him had been defused, had returned to the wilderness of Ziph. Upon hearing of Saul's return, David sent out spies to confirm the rumor, which they did, locating Saul's camp in the process. The report they brought to David was very familiar. As before, Saul had three thousand warriors with him, and he was seeking David's blood.

In the previous encounter with Saul, David and his men were hidden in the sides of a cave that Saul entered unaware. On this occasion, David, along with his companion Abishai, entered the presence of Saul by choice (v. 7). Why there were no guards on duty is a mystery, an issue that David later addressed, rebuking Abner for disregarding his responsibility to keep the king safe (vv. 15-16).

Abishai insisted that God had led them to this place to slay the king, but he didn't encourage David to do it. Instead, he begged for the privilege of doing it himself, boasting that if permitted, he would not have to strike him a second time (v. 8).

David's position, however, had not changed. With every circumstance David faced, he learned more about the character and goodness of his God. He wholly embraced the scriptural principle that God would avenge him, and it was not his responsibility to kill the man that God had placed in authority as king of Israel. His experience in the cave and his thwarted attempt to repay Nabal also served to reinforce his belief. David would have no part of killing Saul, nor would he permit Abishai to do it.

Instead, David took Saul's spear and his "cruse of water" to confirm his presence in Saul's camp and once again demonstrate his benevolent attitude toward the king (v. 11). Standing on a hill overlooking Saul's camp, he first rebuked Abner for failing to protect the king and then turned his attention to Saul, who had recognized his voice, and addressed him personally:

> Wherefore doth my lord thus pursue after his servant? for what have I done? or what evil is in mine hand? Now therefore, I pray thee, let my lord the king hear the words of his servant. If the LORD have stirred thee up against me, let him accept an offering: but if they be the children of men, cursed be they before the Lord; for they have driven me out this day from abiding in the inheritance of the Lord, saying, Go, serve other gods. Now therefore, let not my blood fall to the earth before the face of the Lord: for the king of Israel is come out to seek a flea, as when one doth hunt a partridge in the mountains. (vv. 18–20)

While much of what David said was simply a repetition of his previous conversation with Saul (1 Sam. 24:9–15), there is one notable difference—David no longer referred to Saul as his father. That relationship was established by David's marriage to Saul's daughter Michal. When David became a fugitive, he had to leave her behind and Saul used that opportunity to reclaim her. First Samuel 25:44 tells us that "Saul had given Michal his daughter, David's wife, to Phalti the son of Laish, which was of Gallim."

The rest of David's appeal sounds very familiar. He asked Saul to identify his sin (1 Sam. 26:18). He requested an opportunity to make amends for whatever offense he had committed, and he wondered why Saul believed him to be so great a threat (vv. 19–20). After all, he had only six hundred men, he had no desire to execute the king or take his throne, and he would gladly return and take his place among the servants of Saul.

Genuine repentance bears fruit beyond the expression of sorrow. It is an enduring change of heart that heals and removes the barriers that are damaging the relationship. Saul's confessions never bore even the slightest evidence of authentic repentance.

> Then said Saul, I have sinned: return, my son David: for I will no more do thee harm, because my soul was precious in thine eyes this day: behold, I have played the fool, and have erred exceedingly. (1 Sam. 26:21)

Saul's confession was the insincere, dishonest declaration of a heart fully committed to destroying the man God had chosen to replace him. Nothing he said changed what was in his heart. The only honest thing Saul said was "I have played the fool." Of that, there was no uncertainty.

DISCUSSION QUESTIONS

1. Scripture describes Nabal, a wealthy shepherd living in Maon, as "churlish and evil in his doings" (1 Sam. 25:3). What does that description reveal concerning Nabal's character?
2. It is obvious from 1 Samuel 25:7-8 that David's men had spent some time with Nabal's shepherds. While in their company, they were careful to regard them kindly. Yet when David sent messengers to Nabal seeking provisions, Nabal refused, showing contempt for David and his men. Was David's angry response justified? Was David's angry attitude justified?
3. How was Abigail's mediation used of the Lord to protect David from his own impulsiveness?
4. David had a second encounter with Saul that gave him an opportunity to slay the king. Once again, he refused. How was this encounter different from the previous meeting?
5. For a second time Saul feigned repentance. Did Saul's words reflect the character of his heart? How is genuine repentance revealed in the life of one seeking pardon?

CHAPTER 7
WAITING ON GOD

DAVID'S RESPONSE TO HIS FINAL meeting with Saul was anything but positive. He obviously had no confidence in Saul's promise that he would not harm him.

> David said in his heart, I shall now perish one day by the hand of Saul: there is nothing better for me than that I should speedily escape into the land of the Philistines; and Saul shall despair of me, to seek me any more in any coast of Israel: so shall I escape out of his hand. (1 Sam. 27:1)

Because he was more certain than ever that Saul would exhaust every opportunity to find him and slay him, David once again sought refuge with King Achish at Gath. This time, however, he received a friendly welcome. David was now a confirmed enemy of Saul, even if that wasn't his purpose or desire. He also led a courageous and skilled band of soldiers, men who could prove very valuable to Achish.

David and his men had lived in the city for only a brief period of time before realizing that conditions were less than suitable. His presence in the royal city allowed his actions to be easily observed, requiring much greater caution than he was accustomed to using. Therefore, David requested a different place of residence, one that was somewhat removed from the capital city of Gath. Achish quickly agreed, giving David the city of Ziklag in the southern part of Judah (vv. 5-7). David spent the next sixteen months in the land of the Philistines. Moving provided relief from the pursuit of Saul as well as an opportunity to achieve his primary objective—attacking and destroying the enemies of Israel.

DESTROYING THE ENEMY—1 SAMUEL 27:8–12

The obscurity of a home in Ziklag proved to be of great benefit to David. Even though he was living among the Philistines, who considered him to be their military partner, his loyalties had not changed. He regularly fought battles that he won decisively, delivering huge spoils to Achish in Gath, thereby demonstrating his skill and value as a military leader. When questioned about his activities, he let Achish believe that he was fighting and winning battles against the Israelites in the southern part of Judah, when his victories were, in reality, against the Geshurites, the Gezrites, and the Amalekites, all of whom were allies of Achish and enemies of Israel. For over a year, David managed to attack and destroy Israel's enemies while using those same victories to impress the king of Gath. Achish was convinced that David had become a bitter enemy of Israel—so much so that he believed David had "made his people Israel utterly to abhor him" (v. 12).

There are some who have condemned David for his activities while in Ziklag, saying that his deceitful behavior was beneath his character and implying that there was in David's heart a lack of faith in his God. Yet David's time in Ziklag allowed him to focus directly on the enemy, rather than worrying about Saul, who was not his enemy and against whom he could do nothing. David was still fighting on behalf of Israel while waiting for God to remove Saul from the throne.

FORBIDDEN TO FIGHT—1 SAMUEL 28:1–29:11

God is sovereign. The significance of that statement is almost beyond our comprehension. Nothing happens in the life of one of God's children without His awareness and involvement. *God orchestrates worldly events according to His divine wisdom and directs the movements of men to accomplish His purpose and plan.* It does not matter if men disagree with what He is doing or seek to influence it. God is sovereign, and He will do as He pleases.

Because of his successful exploits and persuasive deception, David soon found himself in an awkward position.

> It came to pass in those days, that the Philistines gathered their armies together for warfare, to fight with Israel. And Achish said unto David, Know thou assuredly, that thou shalt go out with me to battle, thou and thy men. And David said to Achish, Surely thou shalt know what thy servant can do. And Achish said to David, Therefore will I make thee keeper of mine head for ever. (1 Sam. 28:1-2)

The Philistines were preparing for a major battle with Israel in the valley of Jezreel, and there is no doubt that Achish was eagerly anticipating David's participation in the battle. Not only would David and his men provide reinforcement for the Philistine troops, but Achish would also have an opportunity to gloat that Israel's greatest soldier, the one who killed Goliath, was now fighting for him.

We can only imagine how David must have felt when he heard of his new assignment. How would he avoid violating his conscience if he came face to face with Saul on the battlefield? Surely David's heart was filled with anxiety, and the evasive nature of his immediate response reflects that anxiety: "Surely thou shalt know what thy servant can do" (v. 2). Refusing the assignment, however, was not an option.

Meanwhile, Saul was less than eager for a new conflict with the Philistines. His strength and confidence were gone, his courage was gone, and his ability as a military tactician was gone as well. Saul was overwhelmed by the circumstances he faced and had nowhere to turn. Most importantly, God had forsaken him, and like Esau before him, "he found no place of repentance, though he sought it carefully with tears" (Heb. 12:17). So he paid a visit to a woman at Endor who had "a familiar spirit" (1 Sam. 28:7), requesting that she call up Samuel, hoping he would provide some spiritual wisdom—something he could do to improve his standing with God and regain God's guidance. Samuel, rather than providing a way of escape for Saul, condemned Saul for bothering him and reminded him why he was doomed. God is sovereign, and His will had already been determined. There was no recourse for Saul. He was simply reaping what he had sown. He was alone in the darkness of despair, and he was deeply afraid.

As the Philistines prepared for battle, Achish gave orders for David and his men to join him at the rear, thereby fulfilling the responsibility assigned to David in 1 Samuel 28:2 (he was to be the king's bodyguard). While Achish was convinced of David's loyalty to the Philistine cause, the princes (military officers) of the Philistines were not. When they saw David and his men, they strongly objected, demanding that they be removed from their ranks. They were concerned that in the heat of battle, David and his men would show their true loyalties, fighting with Israel and against them. While they acknowledged David to be a fearless soldier, they still considered him their enemy.

What Achish thought didn't matter. His military leaders did not trust David and refused to fight with him in the battle. David had to be dismissed and sent back to Ziklag at once. To maintain his deception and defend his honor, David protested, but once again, his words were a bit vague.

> But what have I done? and what hast thou found in thy servant so long as I have been with thee unto this day, that I may not go fight against the enemies of my lord the king? (1 Sam. 29:8)

David had indeed been fighting against the enemies of his lord the king. Achish understood David to mean that he had been fighting on his behalf, against his enemies, but in reality, David was fighting the enemies of Saul, who was still David's king—the Lord's anointed—and he would never raise his sword against him. So David and his men went home, and the Philistines marched into battle at Jezreel.

Some might think that it was indeed fortunate for David that the "princes of the Philistines" (v. 9) recognized him and refused to go into battle until he was gone. Their demand rescued David from a conflict that would have caused him great anguish of heart. Remaining true to his faith would have required David to turn on the Philistines, destroying the advantage he had gained and putting his men in grave danger. Was it, however, the "princes of the Philistines" who were responsible for David's removal, or were those men simply instruments in the hands of David's God? God is sovereign. *God orchestrates worldly events according to His divine wisdom and directs the movements of men to accomplish His purpose and plan,* and it was His sovereignty that delivered David from fighting against his own people, ensuring that he would not be encouraged to raise his sword against the Lord's anointed.

A STAGGERING DISCOVERY—1 SAMUEL 30:1-31

David must have been greatly relieved to gain exemption from fighting against his own people. Surely the journey back to Ziklag was punctuated with singing and laughter as David and his men considered their good fortune, and it is likely that they gave thanks to God for their deliverance. However, whatever joy they were feeling vanished as they topped the hill and saw their home in the distance. They were greeted by the sight and smell of smoke rising from the ruins of Ziklag.

The Amalekites, the same enemy Saul had been commanded to destroy earlier, were the culprits. The devastation was overwhelming. Not only had David and his men lost their wealth, but their families had been kidnapped as well. So severe was their anguish over the loss that David's men actually discussed stoning him. Whatever distress David felt over Saul's mistrust and pursuit of him paled in comparison with the grief he was experiencing after finding Ziklag in ruins.

David's immediate response was to turn his attention to the One who was in control, the one who had promised that he would be the next king of Israel. He "encouraged himself in the Lord his God" (v. 6). Though he had questions about how to proceed, there was no uncertainty about where he could find the answer.

> David said to Abiathar the priest, Ahimelech's son, I pray thee, bring me hither the ephod. And Abiathar brought thither the ephod to David. And David enquired at the Lord, saying, Shall I pursue after this troop? shall I overtake them? And he answered him, Pursue: for thou shalt surely overtake them, and without fail recover all. (vv. 7–8)

So David and his men began their pursuit of the Amalekites. They got as far as the brook Besor when David realized that two hundred of his men were not strong enough to continue. He left them there and moved forward. As they resumed their journey, they found an Egyptian who was a servant to one of the Amalekites. This slave, who had been left behind because he was sick, agreed to lead David to the enemy's camp in exchange for sparing his life.

The attack was swift and unrelenting. David and his men spent a full twenty-four hours thrashing the Amalekites. When they were finished, they had rescued all their wives and children and recovered everything that had been taken from them. Verse 19 says that "David recovered all."

Several questions come to mind as we contemplate this event in the life of the future king:

- *Why would David leave no men behind to guard Ziklag in his absence?* The Scripture does not say that there were no men there but implies that the Amalekites faced little resistance to their invasion. It is reasonable to assume that David was required by

Achish to present all his skilled soldiers for participation in the battle against Israel, leaving none available to protect the city.
- *How is it that the Amalekites, a ruthless band of invaders and perpetual enemies of Israel, killed no women or children in the battle but instead took them captive?* The only plausible explanation for this is that God in His mercy stayed the hand of the treacherous intruder. The Amalekites were not in the habit of sparing the inhabitants of a city they were looting.
- *Why would David's followers entertain the idea of stoning him?* Leaders are always responsible for choices they make that affect those who follow. While David was, along with his soldiers, a victim (his wives were taken), it was his earlier decisions that were responsible for their calamity. David's men were angry and overwhelmed with grief. They needed someone to blame for their loss, and it was easy for them to point fingers at David.

David's heart was filled with courage, but it was filled with compassion as well. Upon their return to the brook Besor, David and his men were greeted by those who had stayed behind, and there was no doubt great rejoicing as husbands were reunited with their wives and children. What began as a wonderful time of thanksgiving, however, soon became an ugly display of greed.

> Then answered all the wicked men and men of Belial, of those that went with David, and said, Because they went not with us, we will not give them ought of the spoil that we have recovered, save to every man his wife and his children, that they may lead them away, and depart. (v. 22)

It may well have been these same "men of Belial" who were calling for David's death earlier. In any case, they were driven by selfish, sinful appetites, and just as it was easy to blame David for their loss, it was easy to condemn those who were unable to fight.

David's answer came without hesitation:

> Ye shall not do so, my brethren, with that which the Lord hath given us, who hath preserved us, and delivered the company that came against us into our hand. For who will hearken unto you in this matter? but as his part is that goeth down to the battle, so shall his part be that tarrieth by the stuff: they shall part alike. (vv. 23–24)

Though David was not yet king of Israel, he was certainly acting the part. He first gave thanks to God for His preservation and the deliverance of their families as well as their victory over the enemy. Then he established a new ordinance for Israel. They would share equally in any spoil, whether they fought in the battle or guarded the camp, and he would not entertain any other opinions.

David also shared the spoils of this last battle with his brethren in Judah, sending a message with the gift: "Behold a present for you of the spoil of the enemies of the Lord" (v. 26). Like Joshua before him, he was fighting the Lord's battles in a land occupied by the enemy, and he had not forgotten those over whom he was destined to rule.

DISCUSSION QUESTIONS

1. There are many who believe David ignored God's will and demonstrated a lack of faith by fleeing to Gath. They assert that he was acting out of fear rather than faith. Compare David's reaction in 1 Samuel 27:1 with his statement at the end of 1 Samuel 20:3. Was David responding in fear then? Is there a difference between these situations? If so, how are they different?
2. David spent sixteen months living in the land of the Philistines. What evidence, if any, is there that David embraced the culture of the Philistines and forsook the Lord? For whom was David fighting during those months?
3. There is no question that David used deception in dealing with Achish, the king of Gath, while living in Ziklag. Was his deception, in the context of war, a violation of God's law? If so, how did it differ from killing, also in the context of war?
4. In 1 Samuel 29 we are told that David narrowly avoided being forced to fight for the Philistines against Israel. How was David liberated from that risk? Who was responsible for the demand of the Philistine princes that David and his men be sent home?
5. When David and his men returned to Ziklag after being dismissed from the battle, they found their home in ruins. Was this, as some contend, God's judgment for David's lack of faith? If so, why were there no casualties among David's men and their families? Why did God allow David to "recover all" (1 Sam. 30:8)? Is there any evidence of God's displeasure over or condemnation of David's actions while living in Ziklag?

CHAPTER 8

DAVID BECOMES KING

THREE DAYS LATER, DAVID RECEIVED news of the battle at Jezreel, and what he learned caused him great distress. The Philistines had won the battle decisively—it wasn't even close. Once again, the men of Israel fled before the enemy. The Philistines, however, were victorious not because of their larger army or because of their superior skill. They won because God had forsaken Israel's king. Saul's time had come, and the kingdom was no longer his.

KING SAUL IS DEAD—1 SAMUEL 31:1-13

Though it didn't begin that way, Saul's reign was characterized by pride, self-will, and jealousy. When Saul became king, God gave him "another heart" (1 Sam. 10:9). Saul was able to see things differently because God had granted him the presence of His Spirit. Responding to that leadership led to resounding success, which produced popularity with the people, and little by little, Saul's attitude began to change. While it's only natural for effective leaders to be enamored with the praise of men, Saul took it too far. He began to take credit for the victories God gave him on the battlefield. His pride and arrogance led him to believe that he was capable of achieving those victories without God's help. He disobeyed God and then justified his disobedience. Samuel confronted him with his sin and relayed God's message that he would be removed from the throne.

For a while Saul prospered because of David's courage and loyalty, but his jealousy soon destroyed that relationship. At the end of his reign, Saul was lonely, lost, and afraid. After consulting Samuel one last time (calling him up from the grave), he prepared for his final battle.

SAUL'S DEFEAT—1 SAMUEL 31:1–3

The Philistine army was large and powerful, and for Israel the battle started out badly and then got worse. The men of Israel were overwhelmed. Many fled, and those who didn't were slain, including three of Saul's four sons.

Saul was forced to face a brutal reality: "Be sure your sin will find you out" (Num. 32:23). Sin is costly, especially when it involves arrogant rebellion. The Spirit of God had abandoned him; David, his greatest military leader, was no longer available; Samuel, his spiritual adviser, was dead, and now three of his four sons had been slain—all because Saul chose to discount God's will. Saul had "played the fool" (1 Sam. 26:21). Now he was paying the price.

SAUL'S DEATH—1 SAMUEL 31:4–7

Saul's reign began triumphantly and ended tragically. He found himself severely wounded on the battlefield and requested that his armor-bearer take his life, fearing the abuse he would be subjected to should the enemy find him still alive. His armor-bearer, however, like David, was unwilling to raise his hand against God's anointed. Therefore, Saul fell on his own sword, seeking to end his life.

Second Samuel 1 tells us that David learned of Saul's death from an Amalekite who happened on the scene after Saul fell on his sword. The messenger stated that Saul, who was still alive when he arrived, asked him to kill him, which he did (vv. 2–10). Whether Saul died as a result of his attempted suicide or at the hands of the Amalekite cannot with certainty be determined. It is entirely possible that the Amalekite lied. He may well have arrived on the scene after Saul's death and, having taken Saul's crown and bracelet, took them to David, seeking his favor and hoping to receive a reward.

It is especially ironic that the man who brought the news to David was an Amalekite. The Amalekites were those whom God commanded Saul to "utterly destroy," with the added clarification that he was to "spare them not" (1 Sam. 15:3). Yet we know that Saul spared at least one of them. He took Agag the king alive to display as a trophy of his victory. He also spared the best of the spoils in disobedience to God's command, justifying his decision by insisting that he would use them as instruments of worship. God, however, is not interested in our ideas or opinions, and when we choose to keep something God says to destroy, we lay the groundwork for that which we keep to destroy us.

Battles are won when kings are slain. Killing soldiers will discourage the troops, but killing the king demoralizes them. Once Saul was dead, the men of Israel fled en masse, abandoning the cities and leaving them to be taken over by the Philistines.

SAUL'S DISHONOR—1 SAMUEL 31:8-13

The thing that Saul tried to avoid while alive occurred after his death. While the Philistines were not able to torture Saul, they were eager to abuse his body. Having found Saul with his sons lying on the battlefield the next morning, they removed Saul's armor and cut off his head. After they sent messengers throughout the country to report their victory, the armor was sent to the house of Ashtaroth, one of their pagan temples, to be placed on display, the bodies of Saul and his sons were fastened to the wall of Beth-shan, and Saul's skull was tacked up in the temple of Dagon (1 Chron. 10:10).

Many years earlier, soon after he became king, Saul had delivered Jabesh-gilead from an assault by the Ammonites (1 Sam. 11:1–11). To express their gratitude and show honor for their fallen king, the men of that city traveled all night to recover the bodies of Saul and his sons, bringing them back to Jabesh for burial. Then they fasted seven days, showing their respect for them.

DAVID MOURNS SAUL'S DEATH—2 SAMUEL 1:1-27

Finally ten long years of fleeing, agony, homelessness, and uncertainty were over, yet David was in no mood to rejoice. Soon he would be anointed a second time, in a public ceremony, placing him in leadership over Judah. For now, however, David's mind was focused elsewhere. He had received a report from a man, an Amalekite, who claimed he escaped from the camp of Israel and had news of the battle in Jezreel. Saul and Jonathan were dead. How did he know? He was Saul's executioner, and he had the king's crown and bracelet to prove it.

What happened next must have thrust daggers of fear into the heart of the messenger. He was expecting to see David overcome with joy at the news, expressing gratitude for his bravery, perhaps even offering him some reward for his good deed. Instead, David rent his clothes, weeping bitterly over the death of the king and his dear friend Jonathan.

David's tribute to his fallen king and friend Jonathan is found in verses 19-27. It is an unbelievably touching expression of his appreciation for their service and contributions to Israel. In it he encouraged the people of Israel to remember them with gratitude. Though Saul was plagued by many faults and failures, he was still the Lord's anointed—the first king of Israel—and for that, he should be remembered graciously.

The messenger who brought the news, however, received no such grace. He was guilty of slaying the Lord's anointed (or, at the very least, stripping his dead body), and he paid for it with his life.

DAVID BEGINS HIS REIGN—2 SAMUEL 2:1-32

Now David faced an unfamiliar situation; he no longer had to hide from Saul. He was free to return to his homeland, but where exactly should he go? Upon receiving clear direction from the Lord, he moved to Hebron, a major city in Judah about twenty miles from Jerusalem. There David was anointed king.

Still, the throne that David accepted was not the one that Saul occupied. Saul reigned over a united Israel from his home in Gibeah. David was reigning over part of a nation with divided loyalties. Abner, the captain of Saul's army, had taken Ishbosheth, Saul's only surviving son, to Mahanaim to establish him as king of Israel, creating a national disunion that would last for seven and a half years.

For ten years David's character had been tested. His suffering and hardship had helped him mature as a leader, preparing him for what he was yet to face. Many of the psalms that he wrote were composed during those times of testing, and the principles he learned would be vital to his effectiveness as king. Psalm 121, though not officially attributed to David, certainly reflects his thinking regarding the source of his much-needed help:

> I will lift up mine eyes unto the hills, from whence cometh my help. My help cometh from the Lord, which made heaven and earth. He will not suffer thy foot to be moved: he that keepeth thee will not slumber. Behold, he that keepeth Israel shall neither slumber nor sleep. The Lord is thy keeper: the Lord is thy shade upon thy right hand. The sun shall not smite thee by day, nor the moon by night. The Lord shall preserve thee from all evil: he shall preserve thy soul. The Lord shall preserve thy going out and thy coming in from this time forth, and even for evermore. (vv. 1–8)

David's first act as king of Judah was to send a message of gratitude to the men of Jabesh-gilead for their kindness to Saul's family. Their courage in the face of danger was commendable; that they risked their lives to honor Saul *after* his death was worthy of special recognition. Instead of focusing on his newfound authority as king, David chose to center his attention on those who had been kind to the former king.

WAR WITH ISRAEL—2 SAMUEL 2:12–17

Abner, the captain of Saul's army, was responsible for the division in Israel. He refused to acknowledge David as king, instead seeking to revive the reign of Saul in the person of Saul's lone surviving son, Ishbosheth. To accomplish his goal, he gathered his forces and marched on Gibeon. Doing so was essentially a declaration of war on David.

The confrontation took place at the pool of Gibeon. Abner, leading the army of Israel, was on one side, and Joab, fronting David's men, was on the other. The battle began, at Abner's suggestion, with a contest between twelve soldiers from each side. "Let the young men now arise, and play before us" was how Abner characterized the event. This "game" that they "played" resulted in the bloody deaths of twenty-four men. From that day forward, the place was called Helkathhazzurim, meaning "plot of the sharp blades."[9]

Rather than settling the matter, the contest became the impetus for a full-scale battle. Though Abner's force was much larger (he had the support of every tribe in Israel except Judah), they were no match for David's men.

THE DEATH OF ASAHEL—2 SAMUEL 2:18–24

Zeruiah, David's sister (1 Chron. 2:16), had three sons: Abishai, Joab (the captain of David's army), and the youngest, Asahel, who "was as light of foot as a wild roe" (2 Sam. 2:18). Driven by the emotion of a victorious rout, Asahel singled out Abner and pursued him as he was fleeing the battle.

Whether he was acting out of some military obligation or simply indulging his youthful zeal, we are not told. We are told that Abner had no desire to harm Asahel. He knew that killing him would only deepen an already-hostile rivalry with Asahel's brother Joab, so he encouraged him twice to turn aside. Because Asahel was no match for Abner in fighting skill, the wise move would have been to take Abner's advice. Instead, Asahel continued his pursuit. Killing Abner would disorient Israel's army and earn Asahel some much-desired esteem in the eyes of his brother Joab. When he refused to turn aside, Abner stopped suddenly, allowing Asahel to run on the back of Joab's spear, piercing him "under the fifth rib" and killing him (v. 23).

Abner continued his flight—only now there were two chasing him, Joab and Abishai, seeking to avenge their brother's death.

ABNER CALLS FOR A CEASE-FIRE—2 SAMUEL 2:25-32

Circumstances can easily change an individual's perception and shift his priorities. Abner, who began the day challenging Joab to a battle, finished the day standing on a hill negotiating peace.

> Then Abner called to Joab, and said, Shall the sword devour for ever? knowest thou not that it will be bitterness in the latter end? how long shall it be then, ere thou bid the people return from following their brethren? (v. 26)

It appears that Abner's primary concern was that continued war would only intensify the bitterness that already existed between Judah and the rest of Israel, and he was unhappy that Joab was prolonging the war. But Joab didn't start the conflict—Abner did, and it wasn't the bitterness of national division that motivated his request, nor was he concerned about prolonged bloodshed. While Abner was a brash, opportunistic commander, he was pragmatic as well. When he finally managed to reunite with his troops, Abner learned they had lost 360 men, a staggering number considering the overwhelming advantage they had. Besides, the unfortunate death of Asahel had made the battle personal; he now had a much larger target on his back.

Joab's response clarified the issue: "As God liveth, unless thou hadst spoken, surely then in the morning the people had gone up every one from following his brother" (v. 27). In other words, if Abner had not challenged Judah, they would have gone home that morning. One commentary explains Joab's response this way: "Thus Joab threw all the blame of the fight upon Abner, because he had been the instigator of the single combat; and as that was not decisive, and was so bloody in its character, the two armies had felt obliged to fight it out."[10] Joab then blew a trumpet, the battle ended, and the armies returned to their homes.

As Judah began their journey home, Joab tallied the casualties. Judah had lost twenty soldiers, including Asahel, to Israel's 360. God was indeed helping David.

DISCUSSION QUESTIONS

1. First Samuel 31 details Saul's final battle against the Philistines. Saul entered the battle alone, and Samuel had made it clear that he could expect no help from the Lord. What factors led to Saul's spirit of isolated desperation?
2. Why was it significant that the messenger who brought news of Saul's death to David was an Amalekite?
3. How did David's love for and loyalty to King Saul influence his attitude toward Saul's death?
4. The men of Jabesh-gilead exerted great effort to recover the bodies of Saul and his three sons to give them a proper burial. What motivated those men to show such respect for their fallen king? How did David react to their kind treatment of King Saul and his sons?
5. How did the throne David inherited differ from the throne Saul occupied? What criteria did David use to determine where to establish his royal residence?
6. As the new king of Judah, David found himself facing opposition from a reestablished throne in Israel. Who was the self-appointed leader of that opposition? What motivated this leader's initial confrontation, and why did he later change his approach?

CHAPTER 9

A UNIFIED CROWN

DAVID, WHOSE POLITICAL AND MILITARY strength had increased dramatically, was now well established in Judah, but his struggles were far from over. Conflict with Israel had continued, in spite of Abner's contention that he favored peace, and Ishbosheth still refused to acknowledge the authority of David. The bitter rivalry between Abner and Joab continued to intensify as well, and things were going to get much worse before they got better.

ABNER'S DEFECTION AND DEATH—2 SAMUEL 3:6-39

Abner was a courageous military leader, but he was also a shrewd politician, and his choices were often determined by the size of the benefit he received rather than the strength of his character. Loyalty was expendable, as were honesty and honor. While Abner publicly proclaimed support for Ishbosheth, he was carefully plotting his overthrow. He knew that it was only a matter of time before David controlled all Israel, and his pathway to survival ran through David rather than Ishbosheth. Once an opportunity presented itself, Abner would be gone.

CONFLICT WITH ISHBOSHETH—2 SAMUEL 3:6-11

Abner's opportunity came when Ishbosheth challenged him regarding a breach in royal protocol. Ishbosheth accused Abner of appropriating a member of Saul's harem (Rizpah) for himself. Though Abner's guilt or innocence is not disclosed, such a violation would not be out of character, and if he was indeed guilty, Ishbosheth was justified in objecting. Sleeping with any of the king's wives was considered to be an act of treason. Abner, rather than answering the charges directly, did what he always did when attacked; he dodged and then counterattacked.

> Then was Abner very wroth for the words of Ishbosheth, and said, Am I a dog's head, which against Judah do shew kindness this day unto the house of Saul thy father, to his brethren, and to his friends, and have not delivered thee into the hand of David, that thou chargest me to day with a fault concerning this woman? So do God to Abner, and more also, except, as the Lord hath sworn to David, even so I do to him; To translate the kingdom from the house of Saul, and to set up the throne of David over Israel and over Judah, from Dan even to Beersheba. (vv. 8-10)

In Abner's mind the accusation was more an indication of ingratitude than concern for wrongdoing. Had he not preserved the house of Saul by positioning Ishbosheth as king and defending him against David? Was he not Ishbosheth's closest adviser and the commander of his troops? Was it not reasonable to expect a certain amount of latitude in his behavior because of the benefits his support afforded Ishbosheth?

Abner concluded his heated response with an oath. He "vowed to Ishbosheth's face that he would henceforth espouse the cause of David, and soon bring it to a successful issue."[11]

Now it was Ishbosheth's turn to respond, but he had neither the moral fortitude of the prophet Samuel nor the popularity of his father, Saul, nor the courage of the future king, David. He was little more than a weak, cowardly puppet on the throne, and the overpowering fear in his heart sealed his lips.

NEGOTIATIONS WITH DAVID—2 SAMUEL 3:12-21

Abner wasted little time putting his plan in motion. He contacted David through messengers, implying that David had a legal right to all the land that Israel possessed and offering his assistance in seeing that David acquired it.

He knew that David, because he was both kind and desirous of peace, would likely be open to such an offer.

By this time David had been king of Judah for more than seven years (2 Sam. 5:5). Though he was ready for things to move forward, he was cautious about getting ahead of God. He was open to Abner's proposition with one condition—his wife Michal must be returned to him. Such a condition had both personal and political aspects associated with it.

Royal marriages in Old Testament society were not commonly established as a result of romantic attraction. Instead, they were used as bargaining tools in agreements and alliances between kings and nations. Procuring many wives from different countries demonstrated a king's far-reaching influence and power.

Michal became David's wife as a result of Saul's desire to ensnare him, yet we know that Michal loved David (1 Sam. 18:20-21), and it is safe to assume that David loved her. When Saul's trap failed and David had to flee, Saul gave Michal to Phalti, the son of Laish (1 Sam. 25:44). Now David was demanding that she be returned to him, and fulfillment of the request would establish the legitimacy of his throne.

Though David's agreement was with Abner, it was Ishbosheth alone who had power to grant the request. When David contacted him, the king responded without delay, granting David's request and inadvertently facilitating the end of his reign.

Before making his way to Hebron, Abner paid a visit to the elders of Israel and the leaders of Benjamin, convincing them that the future of Israel would be more secure with David on the throne. David was God's choice and he had God's blessing. The elders of Israel were ready for the change, having "in times past" sought for David's leadership (2 Sam. 3:17). Because Saul was of the tribe of Benjamin, Abner took special care to gain their support, thereby avoiding the danger of provoking their jealousy and opposition.

Abner was a skillful diplomat. Once the negotiations were finalized, all Israel came with "one heart to make David king" (1 Chron. 12:38). David's troops grew to more than 340,000, including 3,000 from the tribe of Benjamin, all of whom were "men of war, that could keep rank"—men who came with hearts that were "perfect" (v. 38).

CONFRONTATION WITH JOAB—2 SAMUEL 3:22-27

Although David had accepted Abner's offer of support, Joab's attitude had not changed. He was still consumed with bitterness over the death of his brother Asahel, and the fact that David had engaged in peaceful negotiations with Abner was unacceptable to him. Joab confronted the king, condemning him for his failure to punish Abner, insisting that he could not be trusted. When David failed to respond, he determined to take matters into his own hands.

Joab sent messengers to Abner, requesting an opportunity to speak with him. Surprisingly Abner agreed and returned to Hebron with the couriers. Once he was there, Joab lured him to a private place "aside in the gate" and "smote him there under the fifth rib, that he died," exacting revenge "for the blood of Asahel his brother" (v. 27). Though Joab accused Abner of being untrustworthy, it was he who practiced deceit.

Joab served as David's general, but he had learned little from his king about dealing with injustice. David spared Saul twice, refusing to take vengeance, even though he was being pursued by Saul. David understood that God would in His time impose justice. Joab acted out of anger, murdering Abner, while Abner killed Asahel in self-defense after warning him twice.

DAVID MOURNS THE DEATH OF ABNER—2 SAMUEL 3:28-39

When David heard what Joab had done, he was overwhelmed with sorrow, publicly mourning Abner's death. He first made sure everyone knew that Joab had acted alone, without his approval. He then pronounced a curse on the house of Joab. Finally, he required Joab and all his followers to publicly mourn the death of Abner.

Joab's actions created a number of issues that caused concern for David:

1. Abner was the key to the peaceful transition of leadership in Israel. With him gone, there was uncertainty about the validity of the negotiations, and it opened the door for additional trouble, which soon came.
2. David had given Abner immunity for his crimes against Judah in exchange for delivering the rest of Israel. Joab had violated that agreement, triggering suspicion toward David among those who were aware of the agreement, even though Joab acted without David's approval.
3. David was dismayed over losing a valiant military commander.

David's concluding remarks regarding this incident are found at the end of 2 Samuel 3:39: "The Lord shall reward the doer of evil according to his wickedness." Many years later, Joab would face the moral consequences of his vicious cruelty in shedding Abner's blood (1 Kings 2:28-34). He would be executed to "take away the innocent blood, which Joab shed" when he killed Abner (v. 31) from Solomon and from the house of David.

THE DEATH OF ISHBOSHETH—2 SAMUEL 4:1-12

The last thing David wanted was to gain the throne as a result of an act of treason, but that's exactly what happened. Ishbosheth was slain in his bedchamber by two men of the tribe of Benjamin, Baanah and Rechab, both of whom served as leaders in Israel's army.

While it is impossible to know with certainty what motivated these assassins, it seems reasonable to assume that they were fully aware of the negotiations taking place between Abner and David. They also understood that Ishbosheth was no more than a puppet king. He would be lost without the guidance of Abner, leaving Israel vulnerable to a swift and certain takeover by David. Rather than face the probable consequences of such a takeover, they decided that their best choice was to do something to gain favor with the new king. So "they brought the head of Ishbosheth unto David to Hebron, and said to the king, Behold the head of Ishbosheth the son of Saul thine enemy, which sought thy life; and the Lord hath avenged my lord the king this day of Saul, and of his seed" (v. 8).

Surprises that reveal our mistakes are never pleasant, and Baanah and Rechab were in for a big surprise. David did not thank them, nor did he express joy at their efforts to help God protect him. Instead, he advised them that it was not them but God who had redeemed his soul "out of all adversity" (v. 9). He also informed them of what happened to the last individual who claimed to have killed the king of Israel.

> When one told me, saying, Behold, Saul is dead, thinking to have brought good tidings, I took hold of him, and slew him in Ziklag, who thought that I would have given him a reward for his tidings: How much more, when wicked men have slain a righteous person in his own house upon his bed? shall I not therefore now require his blood of your hand, and take you away from the earth? (vv. 10–11)

For those who knew David well, his response came as no surprise. Never had David felt the need to "help" God protect him, and he would not disregard the sins of those who did. David gave the command, and Baanah and Rechab were executed. Their hands and feet, symbols of their treason, were hung over a pool in Hebron to demonstrate David's displeasure and their humiliation.

David's long wait was over. Ten years in exile and more than seven years reigning over the tribe of Judah had come to an end. God had removed Saul's family from the throne through the course of natural events, and David had remained faithful. Now Israel was waiting—and David was ready.

DAVID'S THIRD ANOINTING—2 SAMUEL 5:1-25

All David's political opponents were now dead. Saul and all his sons had been killed, along with Saul's longtime military captain, Abner. The only remaining heir of the house of Saul was Mephibosheth, the son of Jonathan, who was injured when his nurse dropped him while fleeing from the Philistines (2 Sam. 4:4). Israel was without a leader, and the house of Saul provided no successor to the throne.

DAVID IS ANOINTED KING—2 SAMUEL 5:1-5

Twice before, David had been anointed king of Israel—the first time by the prophet Samuel in a private ceremony in Bethlehem, the second time by the men of Judah in a public ceremony in Hebron. Now he was approached again, this time by a formal delegation of the elders of the remaining eleven tribes of Israel. They came seeking an alliance with him, listing three reasons for their request:

1. "We are thy bone and thy flesh" (v. 1). Though David was not of the tribe of Benjamin nor related to Saul directly, he was still a Jew, which qualified him for the throne of Israel. That he had become widely popular while serving in Saul's court made them feel that much closer to him.
2. "Also in time past, when Saul was king over us, thou wast he that leddest out and broughtest in Israel" (v. 2). Even though Saul was their king, the people knew that it was David who was responsible for their military success. He had proven himself on the battlefield, and Israel's soldiers were eager to follow his leadership.
3. "The Lord said to thee, Thou shalt feed my people Israel, and thou shalt be a captain over Israel" (v. 3). This was by far the most compelling reason for their request. Abner had said the same earlier in his negotiations with them (2 Sam. 3:18). If these elders did indeed understand the legitimacy of that testimony, they were pronouncing an indictment against themselves. Why did they wait so long? Their proposal that Israel make a league with David was long overdue.

The elders anointed David a third time. He had been toughened by the afflictions he endured while in exile, matured by the difficulty of the many personal trials he faced, and molded by the hand of God for this very moment. *God orchestrates worldly events according to His divine wisdom and directs the movements of men to accomplish His purpose and plan.* David was now thirty-seven years old and the years of waiting were over. He was king of Israel.

DAVID CONQUERS JERUSALEM—2 SAMUEL 5:6-12

The first order of business for the new king was to consolidate the government. Flanked by Benjamin to the north and Judah to the south, Jerusalem was a perfect location for the capital of the newly united nation. The city was bordered on three sides by deep, treacherous ravines, providing a strong fortress for Israel's army. Though Israel had claimed the city right after Joshua died (Judges 1:8), the stronghold (the military fortress on Mount Zion) was still held by the Jebusites.

When David made his way to Jerusalem, he found an enemy that was both arrogant and self-deceived. They taunted the Israelites by warning them to beware of "the blind and the lame" that were protecting the fortress (v. 6). David played their game, challenging his men to smite "the lame and the blind," and offering a military promotion to whoever was successful (v. 8). Among those who took up David's challenge was Joab, who became the captain of the newly formed host of Israel by being the first to enter the fortress (1 Chron. 11:6). David took the stronghold, fortified the city, and established his residence there.

As David began to prosper in Jerusalem, a friendly relationship developed with Hiram, king of Tyre. Tyre, a Phoenician city located on the Mediterranean coast about one hundred miles northwest of Jerusalem, was a center for shipping and commerce and home to many excellent artisans and craftsmen. Hiram, who initiated the friendship, freely provided materials and workmen to build David's palace. His friendship extended beyond David's reign to

David's son Solomon as well, for whom he provided assistance constructing the temple (1 Kings 5:1–12).

DAVID BATTLES THE PHILISTINES—2 SAMUEL 5:17–25

David spent sixteen months living with his men and their families in Ziklag, and while Achish considered him to be an ally, David had continued to fight on behalf of Israel. When he took his men to Hebron and became king of Judah, the Philistines took little notice. At that point David still had a small army and posed little threat. When they learned, however, that all Israel was uniting under David's leadership, they became concerned. They knew all too well David's strength, wisdom, and leadership ability, and they were determined to keep Israel from gaining supremacy in the region, so they came looking for David, intending to kill him.

The Philistines staged their attack in the valley of Rephaim. David responded by first seeking guidance from the Lord, asking two questions: (1) "Shall I go up to the Philistines?" and (2) "Wilt thou deliver them into my hand?" (v. 19). Upon receiving affirmative answers to both questions, David proceeded to Baalperazim, where he won a decisive victory, collecting their abandoned idols in the process. First Chronicles 14:12 states that the Philistines "had left their gods there," and David disposed of them by burning them, as instructed by Jewish law (Deut. 7:5, 25).

The Philistines, however, were not finished. They returned a second time to the valley to confront Israel. David again sought direction from God, but this time the Lord instructed David to embrace a different plan. He was not to confront them directly. Instead, he was to outflank them, surprising them from the rear. As before, Israel won a great victory, smiting the Philistines "from Geba until thou come to Gazer" (2 Sam. 5:25).

DISCUSSION QUESTIONS

1. Abner had aligned himself with Ishbosheth, Saul's only surviving son, and supported his installation as king of Israel. Was Abner's loyalty sincere? How did Abner's attitude change as Judah became stronger under David's leadership? What specific event seemed to intensify Abner's determination to move in a different direction?
2. How did David respond when Abner approached him, offering assistance in uniting Israel under David's leadership? What condition did David place on such an agreement? How did David demonstrate respect for King Ishbosheth in the process?
3. How did Abner die? Was his death justified? Is anger ever a valid motivation for a violent response?
4. What was David's reaction to Abner's death? How did Abner's death affect the pending unification of Israel?
5. How did Ishbosheth die? Those who were responsible for his death assumed their actions would please the new king. What did they learn about David's character when they presented their "gift" of deliverance to the king?
6. What factors led the elders of the delegation from Israel to pursue an alliance with David? How did the sovereignty of God affect the events of that day? Does God deal with men and nations in a similar fashion today?

CHAPTER 10

BRINGING THE ARK HOME

A SIN OF CARELESSNESS

ONCE DAVID HAD ESTABLISHED A central location for Israel's government, he set about reinstating their commitment to worship. Many decades had passed since Israel as a unified nation had offered sacrifices in the tabernacle, which still resided in Gibeon. During the reign of Saul, the practice of worship held no place of priority, and instructions given by God held no place of authority. Israel's spiritual life was in horrible disarray, and it was David's desire to see that problem corrected.

DAVID'S MISSION—2 SAMUEL 6:1-2

Jewish law was very specific regarding worship. The tabernacle contained three clearly defined areas: the outer court, the Holy Place, and the holy of holies. The holy of holies was the most sacred of the three, housing the ark of the covenant on which rested the mercy seat. The high priest alone was authorized to enter the holy of holies once a year to sprinkle blood on the mercy seat to atone for the sins of the people.

The ark of the covenant, however, was not in the tabernacle, nor had it been for years. The Philistines had seized it during an assault in the days of Eli (1 Sam. 4:1–7:1). Supposing they had captured a valuable though powerless treasure, the Philistines placed the ark in a house dedicated to their god, Dagon, in Ashdod. The next day they found Dagon lying on the floor prostrate before the ark of God. They returned their god to his place of prominence only to find Dagon's stump lying in front of the ark again the next morning, his head and hands broken off.

Physical afflictions then began appearing among the people, and the men of Ashdod came to a sobering conclusion: "The ark of the God of Israel shall not abide with us: for his hand is sore upon us, and upon Dagon our god" (1 Sam. 5:7). Four other Philistine cities—Gaza, Askelon, Gath, and Ekron—would suffer deadly consequences for unlawfully retaining the ark of God before they finally made the wise choice to take it back to Israel.

The ark finally came to rest in the home of a man named Abinadab, of Kirjath-jearim. He and his sons would shelter and care for the ark for the next seventy years, until David came to take it to Jerusalem.

David's lifelong desire was to build a permanent home for the ark, and though he made plans and gathered the necessary materials for its construction, God did not allow him to do it (1 Chron. 22:2-8). For now he would have to be satisfied with a temporary home for the ark, so David constructed a tabernacle, a tent where all Israel could come to worship their God (1 Chron. 15:1). Then he, along with thirty thousand men, went to Kirjath-jearim to retrieve the ark.

DAVID'S MOTIVE—1 CHRONICLES 13:3

When the Scripture says that David was "a man after [God's] own heart" (1 Sam. 13:14), it means that there were certain things in David's heart that made him unique. David's priorities were determined by his love for God. His heart was wholly focused on his God. His very soul was driven by the pursuit of his God.

> O God, thou art my God; early will I seek thee: my soul thirsteth for thee, my flesh longeth for thee in a dry and thirsty land, where no water is; To see thy power and thy glory, so as I have seen thee

in the sanctuary. Because thy lovingkindness is better than life, my lips shall praise thee. Thus will I bless thee while I live: I will lift up my hands in thy name. My soul shall be satisfied as with marrow and fatness; and my mouth shall praise thee with joyful lips: When I remember thee upon my bed, and meditate on thee in the night watches. Because thou hast been my help, therefore in the shadow of thy wings will I rejoice. My soul followeth hard after thee: thy right hand upholdeth me. (Ps. 63:1–8)

David made three statements in those eight verses that set him apart from an average man, all dealing with the desire of his soul:

1. "My soul thirsteth for thee." (v. 1)

David portrayed himself as a man desperate for water, wandering in a land where none was available. A man enduring such torture would do almost anything to quench his thirst. David's account, however, was more than simply a graphic description of his physical need; it was a metaphor for his real longing, which was the presence and power of God. As a man dying of thirst seeks for water, so David's soul was pursuing his God.

2. "My soul shall be satisfied . . ." (v. 5)

What is required to satisfy the soul of the common man? Achieving success? Gaining wealth? Wielding power? In most cases the answer would involve, in some measure, fulfilling the desires of the flesh. Yet David clearly stated that his satisfaction came from meditating on his God "in the night watches" (v. 6).

3. "My soul followeth hard after thee." (v. 8)

David's message here is that his soul cleaved to his God. It was as if he was glued fast to Him as pieces of wood are glued together. First Samuel 31:2 says that "the Philistines followed hard upon Saul and upon his sons; and the Philistines slew Jonathan, and Abinadab, and Melchishua, Saul's sons." They chased them until they caught them. David was relentless in pursuit of his God.

The driving force of David's heart was a desire to know and honor the Lord. He wanted his words and his meditation to be right: "Let the words of my mouth, and the meditation of my heart, be acceptable in thy sight, O LORD, my strength, and my redeemer" (Ps. 19:14). He wanted to do God's will: "I delight to do thy will, O my God: yea, thy law is within my heart" (Ps. 40:8).

He wanted to exalt the Lord: "I will praise thee, O Lord, with my whole heart; I will shew forth all thy marvellous works" (Ps. 9:1). He wanted to see God's face: "When thou saidst, Seek ye my face; my heart said unto thee, Thy face, Lord, will I seek" (Ps. 27:8). He wanted his spirit to be right: "Create in me a clean heart, O God; and renew a right spirit within me" (Ps. 51:10). In Psalm 108:1 David said, "O God, my heart is fixed; I will sing and give praise, even with my glory."

David's heart was consumed with honoring his God, and bringing the ark to Jerusalem would aid in achieving that goal. In Psalm 26:8 David said, "Lord, I have loved the habitation of thy house, and the place where thine honour dwelleth." The ark was the place of God's habitation on earth, and David wanted all Israel to know the presence of God and honor Him with their worship.

DAVID'S MISTAKE—2 SAMUEL 6:1–11; 1 CHRONICLES 13:1–14

David's mission was right: "Let us bring again the ark of our God to us: for we enquired not at it in the days of Saul" (1 Chron. 13:3). The people of Israel needed a revival. It had been more than seventy years since they had participated in structured worship of any kind. The presence of the ark would make that goal possible.

David's motive was right. His heart was set on honoring his God and encouraging the people of Israel to do the same. He was seeking to provide a proper home for the ark, and he wanted to get it done quickly. Yet in his eagerness and haste, David ignored a crucial biblical principle: God's work must be done according to God's guidelines!

David was far too casual in his approach, and his carelessness was revealed in four areas.

DAVID SEEKS ADVICE FROM THE WRONG PEOPLE

> David consulted with the captains of thousands and hundreds, and with every leader. And David said unto all the congregation of Israel, If it seem good unto you, and that it be of the Lord our God, let us send abroad unto our brethren every where, that are left in all the land of Israel, and with them also to the priests and Levites which are in their cities and suburbs, that they may gather themselves unto us: And let us bring again the ark of our God to us: for we enquired not at it in the days of Saul. And all the congregation said that they would do so: for the thing was right in the eyes of all the people. (1 Chron. 13:1–4)

David consulted the people of Israel, and he moved forward because "the thing was right in the eyes of all the people" (v. 4). It is almost unthinkable that a man whose heart was so consumed with honoring the Lord could forget to consult the Lord he was seeking to please. David got so caught up in the excitement of *what* he was doing that he forgot to ask *how* he was supposed to do it, and his impulsiveness had deadly consequences.

DAVID FOLLOWS THE WRONG EXAMPLE

> They set the ark of God upon a new cart, and brought it out of the house of Abinadab that was in Gibeah: and Uzzah and Ahio, the sons of Abinadab, drave the new cart. (2 Sam. 6:3)

That David chose to place the ark "upon a new cart" may seem trivial, yet Scripture notes it carefully. Why did he make that choice, especially when Jewish law gave specific instructions regarding the transport of the ark that contradicted what he chose to do (Num. 4:4-6)? He followed the example set by the Philistines when they returned the ark to Israel rather than adhering to Jewish law (1 Sam. 6:7-8). In doing so, David demonstrated disrespect that doomed his mission to failure. Doing the right thing for the right reason was not enough; he needed to do it the right way.

DAVID ASSUMES GOD IS PLEASED

> David and all the house of Israel played before the Lord on all manner of instruments made of fir wood, even on harps, and on psalteries, and on timbrels, and on cornets, and on cymbals. (2 Sam. 6:5)

So David and all Israel rejoiced as they brought the ark of God to Jerusalem. Were they honoring God, or were they proud of the fact that they were honoring God? It is surely a fine distinction, but the heart that is truly set on honoring the Lord is careful to show respect not only for the practice that demonstrates worship but also for the will of the object of that worship. There is no value associated with worshipping God on human terms; it must be done according to God's standard.

DAVID REAPS TRAGIC CONSEQUENCES

> When they came to Nachon's threshingfloor, Uzzah put forth his hand to the ark of God, and took hold of it; for the oxen shook it. And the anger of the Lord was kindled against Uzzah; and God smote him there for his error; and there he died by the ark of God. (2 Sam. 6:6-7)

David's joy was shattered when they came to a rough place in the road near Nachon's threshing floor. The oxen stumbled, the cart shook, and the ark began to fall. Uzzah, who along with his brother Ahio was responsible for the safety of the ark, reached out to steady it, which was only logical; but he touched it. As a result, God's anger was kindled, and He killed him.

So who made the mistake? Uzzah? Though he touched the ark, it would not have happened had David taken proper precautions. He was simply doing what he was supposed to do—protect the ark. He was essentially a victim. David made the mistake. His sin of carelessness caused Uzzah's death.

Then three things happened in quick succession: (1) David was displeased with God (v. 8). Imagine that. This man after God's own heart had chosen to pass judgment on his God. His attitude, however, quickly changed. (2) David was afraid of God (v. 9). Fear creates respect, and that respect helped David find the missing element that was hindering his efforts. David finally asked the right question. He had asked, "Is it right to bring the ark to Jerusalem?" He had asked, "Am I right in wanting to bring the ark to Jerusalem?" Now he asked, "*How* shall the ark of the Lord come to me?" (v. 9, emphasis added). (3) David was delayed by God. When the Lord's displeasure became obvious, David made the wise choice to postpone the project.

DAVID'S MODIFICATIONS—2 SAMUEL 6:12-16; 1 CHRONICLES 15:1-29

Three months later, David decided it was time to make another attempt to bring the ark to Jerusalem. As he prepared for this new mission, he clearly did some research. He approached the responsibility with a spirit of reverence that was missing in the first undertaking, and the results reflected the changes. First Chronicles 15 gives the account of the events of that glorious day.

DAVID GATHERS THE LEVITES—1 CHRONICLES 15:2-4

David was not going to make the same mistake twice. He had read the law. Transporting the ark was the exclusive responsibility of the Levites, so he called them together and charged them with retrieving the ark from the house of Obededom, an honor they gladly embraced.

THE LEVITES SANCTIFY THEMSELVES—1 CHRONICLES 15:12-14

In the first attempt, Israel's attitude was somewhat cavalier. They were excited about retrieving the ark, but they failed to give the occasion the respect it was due. Therefore, before they started this mission, the Levites sanctified themselves, making sure there was nothing to hinder God's blessing of their efforts. After they began their journey, having gone only six paces, they stopped to offer a sacrifice, again seeking to make sure that their efforts were acceptable in God's sight (2 Sam. 6:13).

THE LEVITES FOLLOW THE LAW—1 CHRONICLES 15:15-16

The Law contains specific instructions for transporting the ark, a rectangular box made of wood and overlaid within and without with pure gold. Facing each other on top of the box were golden cherubim, and on the bottom of the box were golden rings by which it was to be carried. The Levites were to insert golden rods through the rings and then bear it on their shoulders (Ex. 25:10-18). At no time was any man ever to touch the ark.

GOD HELPS THE LEVITES—1 CHRONICLES 15:26

In verse 13 David told the Levites that Israel's mistake in the first attempt was twofold: first, the Levites did not carry the ark, and second, they failed to seek the Lord's guidance. The result of those errors was that "the Lord our God made a breach upon us." The report was very different on the second attempt. Verse 26 says that "God helped the Levites that bare the ark of the covenant of the Lord." Instead of stopping them, God helped them.

DISCUSSION QUESTIONS

1. One of David's first acts as king of a unified Israel was to reinstate formal worship. What prevented Israel from worshipping according to the ceremonial law? Why was formal worship so important to David?

2. Was David's plan to bring the ark to Jerusalem pleasing in God's sight? Was David's motive right in seeking to do so? Is doing the right thing for the right reason enough to justify moving forward with our plans?

3. Uzzah died when he put forth his hand to keep the ark from falling off the cart as they were moving it to Jerusalem. Was Uzzah's purpose and motive right? If so, why did God kill him? Who was ultimately responsible for Uzzah's death?

4. What was David's initial reaction to Uzzah's death? Was David's attitude toward the Lord justified? How did David's attitude change? What question did David finally ask that significantly aided his mission?

5. David failed because of his carelessness. How was that carelessness revealed in David's approach to moving the ark? In his response to the tragic consequences of his casual attitude?

6. What changes were implemented as a result of David's renewed fear and respect for God?

CHAPTER 11

WHEN KINGS GO FORTH TO BATTLE

A SIN OF COMPLACENCY

COMPLACENCY IS A STRONG WORD. The dictionary defines it as being "a feeling of contentment or self-satisfaction, especially when coupled with an unawareness of danger, trouble, or controversy."[12] While carelessness indicates an attitude of neglect, complacency denotes smugness. People who become complacent are generally comfortable, self-sufficient, independent, and unaccountable. They find it unnecessary to take reasonable precautions to avoid falling into dangerous traps, and the consequences of their transgressions are extensive, affecting family, friends, and followers for the rest of their lives.

DAVID'S SIN

Though David had a godly heart, he still had a sinful nature, which led him to do things that were, for him, uncharacteristic. Yet it was not uncommon for God's faithful servants to have difficulty with sins. Noah got drunk (Gen. 9:20-21). Abraham lied about Sarah, his wife, being his sister, the result of his fear (Gen. 12:10-13; 20:2). Jacob defrauded his brother, Esau, to help God accomplish His will and satisfy his mother (Gen. 27:6-36). Moses became so frustrated with the people God had called him to lead that he struck the rock in anger rather than speaking to it as God had commanded (Num. 20:8–11). All these individuals were guilty of ugly, public sins, yet all were commended for their faithfulness (Heb. 11:7–29). David's sin with Bathsheba was one of those atypical events, the result of his complacency.

At this point in his life, David was about fifty years old and had been king of Israel for some twenty years. His success had mushroomed over the years, providing him with unlimited power, wealth, authority, and influence. Complacency was easy for David.

Some sins come suddenly, a consequence of impulsive, emotional decisions. David made such a mistake when seeking to bring the ark to Jerusalem. Others arrive more gradually, growing silently in the heart over many years without announcing their arrival until it's too late, when the damage has already been done. David's complacency had been growing for many years, aided by his disregard for certain essential elements of the law. God had provided clear guidelines for the lifestyle of Israel's future king while they were wandering in the wilderness:

> When thou art come unto the land which the Lord thy God giveth thee, and shalt possess it, and shalt dwell therein, and shalt say, I will set a king over me, like as all the nations that are about me; Thou shalt in any wise set him king over thee, whom the Lord thy God shall choose: one from among thy brethren shalt thou set king over thee: thou mayest not set a stranger over thee, which is not thy brother. But he shall not multiply horses to himself, nor cause the people to return to Egypt, to the end that he should multiply horses: forasmuch as the Lord hath said unto you, Ye shall henceforth return no more that way. Neither shall he multiply wives to himself, that his heart turn not away: neither shall he greatly multiply to himself silver and gold. (Deut. 17:14–17)

There can be no question that God's plan for Israel's king did not include the practice of polygamy. But what did David do? Second Samuel 3:2–5 says that he enlarged his harem, something that God had clearly forbidden. It identifies six of David's sons, who were born of six different wives. Second Samuel 5:13 speaks of additional, undisclosed numbers of wives and concubines added by David during his time in Jerusalem. Clearly, acquiring wives had become a priority for David.

Because of the distractions, David stayed home at a time "when kings go forth to battle" (2 Sam. 11:1). He was certain that his army was capable of defeating their foe. Yet David was about to confront a different, more subtle enemy, and the battlefield would have been a far less dangerous place for him to be. Second Samuel 11 gives the gruesome details.

DAVID SENDS JOAB TO DESTROY AMMON AND BESIEGE RABAH—2 SAMUEL 11:1

David's problem began when he stayed home. It was the spring of the year, a time when kings resumed battles that were postponed because of the unfavorable conditions afforded by winter weather. In the previous battle against the Syrians, who had come to the aid of the Ammonites, David had led the charge and Israel had slain "the men of seven hundred chariots of the Syrians, and forty thousand horsemen" (2 Sam. 10:18). He was at the pinnacle of his success, and his popularity and power allowed him to operate without accountability. So he stayed home, and no one questioned him.

The rest of the story is very familiar. David was restless that night. Perhaps he was feeling a bit uncomfortable at home in the palace while Joab and Israel's troops were on the battlefield. He had let his desires guide him rather than his wisdom. He arose from his bed and began to stroll on his rooftop, when in the moonlight he saw a beautiful young woman washing herself. The moment he saw her, a battle began in his heart. Would he again allow the desires of his flesh to determine his actions? Passions began to stir in his heart, and he made a choice that would change both his life and his legacy. At this point David had not yet acted on the impulsive desire he was experiencing, but the sin had already taken root in his heart.

DAVID SENDS FOR BATHSHEBA—2 SAMUEL 11:3-4

Ralph Waldo Emerson said, "The ancestor of every action is a thought." While we are not told what David was thinking as he looked at Bathsheba, we can identify his thoughts by his actions.

> David sent and enquired after the woman. And one said, Is not this Bathsheba, the daughter of Eliam, the wife of Uriah the Hittite? And David sent messengers, and took her; and she came in unto him, and he lay with her; for she was purified from her uncleanness: and she returned unto her house. (vv. 3-4)

Two thoughts occupied David's mind. He entertained the possibility of a physical relationship with this beautiful young woman and determined to satisfy his fleshly desire. To that end he sent a message inquiring about her identity. What he learned should have put an end to his pursuit. Her name was Bathsheba. She was the daughter of Eliam and the wife of Uriah the Hittite. Men who are intent on satisfying sensual appetites, however, are seldom swayed by reasonable thoughts. David, at this point, had become a slave to his desires.

If there were any doubts about David's intentions, his second message removed them. David sent messengers to bring Bathsheba to the palace, where this man with a godly heart did the unthinkable—committing adultery with another man's wife. It's hard to imagine how far David had fallen in such a short time. David was feeling exceedingly self-sufficient, and he was very much unaware of the serious implications of his actions—the very essence of complacency.

DAVID SENDS FOR URIAH—2 SAMUEL 11:5-13

Sin has consequences, which are often unexpected and always unpleasant. David learned the unpleasant consequences of his sin with Bathsheba when she sent him a message saying "I am with child" (v. 5). Again, though we are not told what David was thinking, we can discern it from his actions. David began to panic and devised a plan. He would send for Uriah and allow him some time with his wife at home, thereby covering his sin.

Uriah, however, refused to cooperate, sleeping "at the door of the king's house with all the servants of his lord" (v. 9). When David inquired regarding his strange behavior, Uriah made it clear that he did not consider his actions to be strange at all.

> Uriah said unto David, The ark, and Israel, and Judah, abide in tents; and my lord Joab, and the servants of my lord, are encamped in the open fields; shall I then go into mine house, to eat and to drink, and to lie with my wife? as thou livest, and as thy soul liveth, I will not do this thing. (v. 11)

Uriah, unlike David, felt a grave sense of responsibility to his fellow soldiers, and his character would not allow him to enjoy the king's generous offer. He was being guided by principles rather than fleshly appetites.

Uriah's response must have been a stinging rebuke to David, who was simply ignoring what he knew to be right. Yet David was beyond backing out. The sin had occurred and a child had been conceived. He still had to find a way to cover his sin, so David made one more attempt.

This time Uriah was summoned to the king's house for dinner. David's plan was to get Uriah drunk, hoping he would forget his values long enough to provide a cover for David's sin. But even in a drunken stupor, Uriah retained his honor. Once again, he slept with the servants. David would have to find another way to hide his sin.

DAVID SENDS URIAH TO DIE—2 SAMUEL 11:14-25

Even if David had succeeded in getting Uriah to go home and sleep in his own bed, he would not have solved his problem. All David's servants were aware of what was happening. They were subjugated partners in David's sin, messengers facilitating his sensual plans. But David wasn't thinking so clearly. Unaware of the futility of his efforts, David conceived one final, foolproof scheme.

> It came to pass in the morning, that David wrote a letter to Joab, and sent it by the hand of Uriah. And he wrote in the letter, saying, Set ye Uriah in the forefront of the hottest battle, and retire ye from him, that he may be smitten, and die. (vv. 14–15)

David sent a message to Joab ordering him to place Uriah in a perilous position and then leave him exposed to the enemy so that he would be killed. This time David's plan worked, but it was costly. An undisclosed number of Israel's valiant soldiers were killed along with Uriah (v. 17), and David didn't bat an eye. When the messenger returned with news of the casualties, David responded with callous indifference: "Thus shalt thou say unto Joab, Let not this thing displease thee, for the sword devoureth one as well as another" (v. 25). David's values had become so twisted that in his mind multiple deaths were a reasonable sacrifice for concealing his sin.

David was finally able to breathe a sigh of relief—at least Uriah would not be able to testify against him.

DAVID SENDS FOR BATHSHEBA—2 SAMUEL 11:26–27

With Uriah gone, David was ready to wrap things up and get this problem behind him. The only thing left was to protect the honor of Bathsheba and provide legitimacy for the child. So after her seven days of mourning were complete, David sent for Bathsheba, she became his wife and bore their son, and David assumed that this episode in his life was over.

THE COST OF SIN—2 SAMUEL 12:1–12

One of the reasons sin is so devastating is that no one counts the cost. Sin led David down a path of misguided expectations. Not for one moment could David ever imagine his sin would be so costly, nor could he ever anticipate the lifelong consequences of his actions. All he saw was the immediate pleasure his choices would bring, and he probably justified those choices by reminding himself of the sacrifices he had already made.

As we examine those choices we learn several things.

- David assigned every responsibility during this sordid event in his life to someone else—the only thing that David did was commit the sin. Then he simply sat back and watched as his plan was carried out, never stopping to think about the destructive impact of his actions on those who obeyed his orders.
- Once David got entangled in his sin, his thinking became twisted. He was desperate, and desperate people convince themselves that their foolish choices make sense. David actually thought that he had covered his sin. Yet his servants knew what was going on, along with Joab and Bathsheba. Nor is it unreasonable to assume that Ahithophel, David's most trusted counselor who later defected to Absalom (2 Sam. 16:23), knew as well. More importantly, the God of heaven was observing David's motives, thoughts, actions, and responses. Second Samuel 11 concludes with a very grave observation: "But the thing that David had done displeased the LORD" (v. 27). David thought the episode was over, but the dominoes had not even started to fall.
- One sin always leads to another, and David's sins had multiplied—lust, adultery, deception, murder, hypocrisy. David compiled quite a list. While on the outside David appeared to be without remorse, on the inside he was in constant agony. The lies he had told himself were no more convincing than those he told his servants. While he was certain he had hidden his sin from everyone else, he could not convince himself. Psalm 32 describes those months of personal conviction: "When I kept silence, my bones waxed old through my roaring all the day long. For day and night thy hand was heavy upon me: my moisture is turned into the drought of summer" (vv. 3-4). Relief would come only

when David was willing to confess his sin, and for that to happen, God would have to intervene.

A VISIT FROM THE PROPHET—2 SAMUEL 12:1-12

Now that David had dispatched his last messenger and supposedly concealed his sin, it was time for the Lord to send a messenger to David. Nathan had visited David once before to convey God's promise that the throne of Israel would continue forever through David's lineage (2 Sam. 7:12-17). Included in that promise was a commitment that God would never again remove His mercy from the king who sat on the throne, as He did with David's predecessor, Saul. Instead, God said that he would "chasten him with the rod of men, and with the stripes of the children of men" (v. 14).

On this occasion Nathan's visit again contained a promise from God. One that David did not enjoy hearing.

DAVID'S HOLLOW RIGHTEOUSNESS—2 SAMUEL 12:1-6

Nathan had the unfortunate responsibility of confronting David with his sin. It would not do to simply challenge David concerning his transgression, because David, though under conviction, considered his sin to be of minor consequence. Nathan had to approach him in a way that would emphasize the magnitude of his offense. So he told David a story—one that would stir David's anger over the injustice portrayed.

Nathan's story had three main characters: a rich man, a poor man, and a little ewe lamb that belonged to the poor man. The rich man hosted a traveler as his guest, and rather than choose a lamb from his own flock, he took the poor man's lamb, dressed it, cooked it, and served it to his visitor.

David's response, driven by his false righteousness, was harsh and unjust, overstating the seriousness of the man's crime and imposing a sentence that went beyond the parameters of the law.

> David's anger was greatly kindled against the man; and he said to Nathan, As the Lord liveth, the man that hath done this thing shall surely die: And he shall restore the lamb fourfold, because he did this thing, and because he had no pity. (vv. 5-6)

David obviously thought Nathan was relating an actual event. His judgment accurately reflected the teaching of the law found in Exodus 22:1, which states, "If a man shall steal an ox, or a sheep, and kill it, or sell it; he shall restore five oxen for an ox, and four sheep for a sheep." The sentence of death, however, was excessive. Nowhere did Jewish law stipulate death for stealing another man's lamb.

Jesus taught that it is unwise to try to remove the splinter in our brother's eye when there is a beam lodged in our own eye (Matt. 7:3-5). David would have been prudent to observe such a principle. Though the sentence David ordered was meant to purge another man's splinter, it was about to be applied to his own beam.

DAVID'S HORRIFYING REALIZATION—2 SAMUEL 12:7-12

Nathan's story had the desired effect. David was deeply offended that the rich man was so selfish and unkind. Nathan first shared the sobering truth, then explained the application of the story.

Pointing his wrinkled, bony finger in David's face, Nathan boldly declared, "Thou art the man" (v. 7). Instantly David realized that he was the rich man in Nathan's story. Uriah was the poor man, and Bathsheba was Uriah's little ewe lamb. David's heart froze as Nathan began to relate the message God had given him.

First, Nathan reminded David of God's rich blessings on him. Though he didn't deserve it, God made him king over all Israel and Judah, gave him a fine home and large family, and stood ready to honor whatever more David would have requested of Him. Next, Nathan identified David's sin.

> Wherefore hast thou despised the commandment of the Lord, to do evil in his sight? thou hast killed Uriah the Hittite with the sword, and hast taken his wife to be thy wife, and hast slain him with the sword of the children of Ammon. (v. 9)

Finally, Nathan announced David's sentence, which was to be carried out in four phases, all in some way affecting his family. Because David despised the commandment of the Lord and took Bathsheba, Uriah's wife, for himself, God promised that as David had slain Uriah the Hittite with "the sword of the children of Ammon," so the sword would never depart from his house.

Then God promised that David would struggle against evil originating from his own house. Nathan went on to explain that David's wives would become prey for his enemies, and these barbaric attacks would occur in broad daylight for all Israel to see. But the most severe promise of judgment came as a result of David's actions that had "given great occasion to the enemies of the Lord to blaspheme" (v. 14). Because of that, the child that was soon to be born to David and Bathsheba would die.

DAVID'S HUMBLE REPENTANCE—2 SAMUEL 12:13–14

Seldom does a person's attitude change so dramatically in such a short time. David went from railing in anger against another man's sin to cowering in fear from his own sense of shame in a matter of minutes. Nathan's account of David's sin was both accurate and sobering, and David could no longer pretend that others didn't know or that his sin didn't matter.

Nathan delivered his message of condemnation in just four words: "Thou art the man" (v. 7). David's confession was not much longer—only six words: "I have sinned against the Lord" (v. 13). Long statements are not convincing anyway, especially if sincerity is not present. God knows the heart, and David's heart was flooded with guilt and grief.

First John 1:9 says, "If we confess our sins, he is faithful and just to forgive us our sins, and to cleanse us from all unrighteousness." Nathan assured David that God had heard his confession and "put away" his sin (2 Sam. 12:13), and although the law clearly called for death as a consequence for adultery (Lev. 20:10), David's life would be spared. David's forgiveness removed his guilt and restored his relationship with his God, but it could do nothing to reverse the damage his sins had caused or remove their long-term consequences, which were devastating.

The baby that was conceived as a result of David and Bathsheba's secret affair died seven days after it was born. David's son Amnon raped his sister Tamar and was slain in retaliation by his brother Absalom (2 Sam. 13:1–29). Absalom rebelled against his father and tried to steal his throne before being killed by David's general, Joab (2 Sam. 18:14). Adonijah, another of David's sons, was slain at the command of his brother Solomon for asking for the hand of a Shunammite woman named Abishag in marriage (1 Kings 2:17–25).

In addition to all that, David's chief adviser and counselor, Ahithophel, defected to Absalom during his rebellion, and he gave specific advice to Absalom that fulfilled a noteworthy item in Nathan's prophecy concerning David's future troubles.

> Then said Absalom to Ahithophel, Give counsel among you what we shall do. And Ahithophel said unto Absalom, Go in unto thy father's concubines, which he hath left to keep the house; and all Israel shall hear that thou art abhorred of thy father: then shall the hands of all that are with thee be strong. So they spread Absalom a tent upon the top of the house; and Absalom went in unto his father's concubines in the sight of all Israel. And the counsel of Ahithophel, which he counselled in those days, was as if a man had enquired at the oracle of God: so was all the counsel of Ahithophel both with David and with Absalom. (2 Sam. 16:20–23)

Why would Ahithophel desert David in such a time of need? That answer is buried in an obscure genealogy in 2 Samuel 23:

> Eliphelet the son of Ahasbai, the son of the Maachathite, Eliam the son of Ahithophel the Gilonite. (v. 34)

Did you notice the name Eliam in the verse above? Does it sound familiar? It should. Eliam was the son of Ahithophel, and we were introduced to him earlier in our study.

> David sent and enquired after the woman. And one said, Is not this Bathsheba, the daughter of Eliam, the wife of Uriah the Hittite? (2 Sam. 11:3)

Ahithophel was Bathsheba's grandfather!

DISCUSSION QUESTIONS

1. David failed in his first attempt to bring the ark of the covenant to Jerusalem because of a careless approach. His affair with Bathsheba reflected an attitude of complacency. How is complacency different from carelessness? Should believers today be concerned about the danger of complacency?
2. Why did David remain home at a time when it was customary for kings to lead their armies into battle? What scriptural guidelines did David ignore (Deut. 17:14–17)? How did disobedience to those commands feed his complacent attitude?
3. It appears that David thought his sin with Bathsheba was a private matter. He assumed that no one else knew what he was doing and that no one (other than Bathsheba) would be affected by his sin. Is it possible for an individual to sin in isolation? What other people were affected by David's sin? How did David's thinking change as his sin progressed?
4. Sin has a way of stunning us with its consequences. What was David's initial reaction to the prophet Nathan's account of an insensitive rich man's treatment of a poor man? Was the sentence David imposed on the rich man just according to Jewish law?
5. How did David's attitude change when he realized his guilt?
6. Because of the serious nature of David's sin, the consequences were significant. How was David's family affected by his sin?
7. Who was Ahithophel, and why would he desert David?

CHAPTER 12

BASKING IN THE GOLDEN GLOW OF SUCCESS

A SIN OF CONCEIT

EXPERIENCE IS THE BEST TEACHER, or so the proverb says. Sometimes you just have to learn the lesson the hard way. The idea is that the experiences of life provide better training than formal instruction or books. It would be wonderful if that was true, but it's not. You would naturally think that older believers would have a closer walk with the Lord and that their vulnerability to temptation would be greatly reduced. Yet many of God's most faithful servants committed their most serious sins late in life when they should have known better.

Noah, a man who is commended because he "walked with God" (Gen. 6:9), was over six hundred years old when he got drunk *after* God had delivered his family from the flood (Gen. 9:20–21). Moses had been walking with God for over seventy years when he struck the rock rather than speaking to it as God commanded, displaying his unbelief (Num. 20:8–11). Joshua was at least in his sixties when he displayed presumption and overconfidence in his attack on Ai (Josh. 7:2–4).

David had been king for nearly forty years. His experiences were vast and varied, having enjoyed the pleasure of God's blessing as well as the pain of

God's chastening. He had learned the importance of respect for God the hard way, suffering the consequences of careless disrespect. Those experiences should have prepared him to face the gravest of temptations.

THE ROOT OF SIN

The event we are going to examine occurred immediately after David's final recorded battle, a notable victory over the Philistines (2 Sam. 21:15-22). In David's first battle he was an inexperienced youth, essentially unfit for warfare; in his last battle he was an accomplished man of war. In his first battle he fought against a Philistine giant named Goliath; his final battle was also against a Philistine giant. In his first battle David battled alone with a sling and five smooth stones; in his final battle he commanded an army of highly skilled soldiers numbering over one million (2 Sam. 24:9). David's first battle was against impossible odds, and David was totally dependent on the Lord for victory; in his final battle he was by far the dominant force, and victory was all but assured.

Now David's battles were over, and he had time to reflect on what God had done in his life. Immediately after his victory, he composed a song of praise to the Lord (2 Sam. 22). In it he reflected on God's abundant blessing on his reign, remembering His character and expressing gratitude for His grace and guidance. David also took care to rejoice that God had subdued all his enemies before him (vv. 38-49), and according to verse 45, even strangers were submitting to his authority. David had truly become the master of his world.

DAVID'S CONCEIT—2 SAMUEL 24:1-9

Why David chose to take a census immediately after such an overwhelming victory is a mystery. If his purpose was to collect the atonement offering for the service of the tabernacle as detailed in Exodus 30:11-16, there would have been no offense. The other common purpose for a census was to enroll additional soldiers in the army. However, the success of Israel's recent military campaigns brought widespread peace, making that unnecessary.

It seems likely that David was simply celebrating his profound success as king of Israel, and the acclaim for that success slowly transitioned from God to David. He was not seeking to enlist new soldiers; he simply wanted to know how many prospects were available. Joab knew it was wrong and questioned the king's decision (2 Sam. 24:3), but David would not be deterred. For the next nine months and twenty days, Joab and his aides crisscrossed Israel and Judah, gathering information about those men who were legitimate candidates for military service. Finally they delivered the staggering number to the king. In Israel alone, there were eight hundred thousand warriors available, and in Judah, five hundred thousand. An army of more than 1.3 million put David in a position of overwhelming military dominance. David had forgotten the source of his success, and for that, he was about to pay dearly.

DAVID'S CONFESSION—2 SAMUEL 24:10

David's godly heart was most evident in situations where he had done things that were ungodly. As before, David did not delay acknowledging his sin.

> David's heart smote him after that he had numbered the people. And David said unto the Lord, I have sinned greatly in that I have done: and now, I beseech thee, O Lord, take away the iniquity of thy servant; for I have done very foolishly. (v. 10)

Genuine confession is more than remorse or sorrow for having done something wrong. It is a clear understanding of the evil of our offense coupled with a spirit of humility. There can be no effort to avoid responsibility for or justify what we have done. David openly acknowledged his sin, characterizing it as foolish iniquity and sincerely seeking God's forgiveness.

DAVID'S CHASTISEMENT—2 SAMUEL 24:11-17; 1 CHRONICLES 21:9-17

Once again, David received a visit from a prophet. Gad brought a message of judgment from the Lord, offering David three choices. The first was a famine in the land that would last three years. The second option had a much shorter duration, only three months, but David would be at the mercy of his enemies. The unspoken message was that David's massive army was of no value whatsoever without the blessing of God. The third option would last only three days but would involve massive destruction "throughout all the coasts of Israel" (1 Chron. 21:12).

David based his decision on who was administering the punishment. He determined that he would prefer to trust the mercy of his God rather than experience the brutality of his enemies. David had no idea what was coming. The results were crushing. A deadly pestilence overshadowed the nation of Israel, and seventy thousand men died. It would have been more, except that God's mercy prevailed when the angel began to lift his hand of destruction over Jerusalem.

As a result, David's kingdom was considerably smaller, and David's pride was shattered. Once again, he confessed his sin, acknowledging the seriousness of what he had done and pleading for God's mercy on behalf of the people. Since he was the one guilty of the crime, he requested that he be allowed to take the punishment.

DAVID'S CONSECRATION—2 SAMUEL 24:18–25

The prophet Gad had one more message for David. He was to erect an altar to the Lord at the place where the judgment of God was stayed—Araunah's threshing floor. By this time David's focus was crystal clear; he was determined to be obedient, and he wanted to be reconciled to his God, so he "went up as the Lord commanded" (v. 19).

As David approached, Araunah came out to meet him. Recognizing the king, he bowed before him and inquired as to the reason for his visit. David mentioned three objectives, each dependent on the fulfillment of the previous one. He wanted to buy Araunah's threshing floor so that he could build there an altar to the Lord, which would allow him to offer the atonement necessary to stop the plague.

The conversation that followed was unusual. Araunah began by offering to give David everything he needed. The property itself, the materials necessary for the construction of the altar, and the oxen for the sacrifice were all included in the gift. David, however, was unwilling to accept such a gift. To offer a sacrifice on that basis would have been, for David, no sacrifice at all. A sacrifice must come at a cost to the one offering the sacrifice; therefore, David insisted on purchasing the things he requested.

The agreed-on amount was "fifty shekels of silver" (v. 24). (The purchase price mentioned in 1 Chronicles 21:25, "six hundred shekels of gold by weight," is easily explained. David first bought the threshing floor proper along with the necessary items for the sacrifice for the lesser amount. Later, when he was making preparation for building the temple, more land was needed. The larger amount reflects the purchase price at that time.)

David made the purchase, built the altar, and offered the sacrifice. "So the Lord was intreated for the land, and the plague was stayed from Israel" (1 Sam. 24:25).

THE IMPACT OF SIN

> Then when lust hath conceived, it bringeth forth sin: and sin, when it is finished, bringeth forth death. (James 1:15)

This was David's third notable sin. While it is certain that there were others, God chose to use these three to illustrate the scope, significance, and sorrow of sin. Every sin is "conceived" in the heart by lust and "bringeth forth death," but every sin is not the same, and human consequences vary depending on the severity of the sin.

Though forgiveness through the sacrifice of our Savior eliminates the eternal penalty for our sin, the law of sowing and reaping still operates on a temporal level. Outside of divine intervention, men, even believers, still suffer the effects of selfish choices and foolish desires. David's three sins provide valuable wisdom concerning the truth of that principle.

David's first sin was the result of careless enthusiasm. He was the newly anointed king of Israel, and his sincere desire was to honor his God by bringing the ark to Jerusalem. While what David did was without question sinful, it was not premeditated. He simply failed to take the time to prepare properly for what he was going to do. As a result of David's sin, a man lost his life. Uzzah died not because of intentional sin on his part. David had sown the seed responsible for Uzzah's needless death.

David's second sin occurred after he had been on the throne for twenty years. While David's sin with Bathsheba sprang from the impulsive desires of his heart, there was nothing impulsive about the sin itself. Not only did David plant the seed; he also watered it well and nurtured it to full maturity. His extensive efforts to conceal what he had done left no doubt as to his guilt, and the consequences reflected the serious nature of his transgression. Five individuals—Uriah, the baby, and three of David's sons—died because of his sin, along with several other brave soldiers.

David's third sin occurred after he had been ruling for almost forty years. Aging is supposed to enhance wisdom, making foolish mistakes less probable. Yet David's most grievous sin happened at the end of his life. Having just won a great victory, David decided to number the people, gaining impressive stats to demonstrate his power and might. There was nothing impulsive or accidental about this sin. David was acting with brazen arrogance, and as a result, seventy thousand men died.

Each sin got worse. Each sin evoked greater punishment, and each time, David should have known better.

DISCUSSION QUESTIONS

1. Although there were surely others, the Bible records three notable sins in David's life. What was David's third sin, and how was it different from the first two? What motivated his sin?
2. David had been king of Israel for nearly forty years when he committed this final sin. What impact did age have on his decision?
3. Why is this sin more disappointing than the other two?
4. For the first time God gave David the opportunity to choose his punishment. What factors affected David's choice? How did David's choice reflect the sincerity of his repentance?
5. How was the nation of Israel different after God's punishment was inflicted? How had David changed?
6. What significant lesson is taught in 2 Samuel 24 regarding the nature of sacrifice?
7. David's experiences with sin clearly teach that some sins are worse than others. How would you characterize the difference in David's sins? How did God's choice of punishment reflect the severity of each sin?

CHAPTER 13

DEALING WITH GUILT

THE STORY IS TOLD THAT a famous playwright once played a prank on ten well-known men in London. He wrote each of them an identical anonymous letter that said, "We know what you have done; if you don't want to be exposed, leave town." Within six months, all ten men who received the letter moved!

Guilt is a powerful emotion that affects people in dreadful ways. It is not unusual to find guilty individuals filled with despair and unable to function normally. Often the anguish is so severe that chronic physical illness becomes a reality. Reasoning abilities are hampered and flawed thinking leads to tragic, life-changing decisions.

Guilt is also a potent tool that others can use to control people. Every blackmail scheme ever devised had guilt at its core. Left to do its work in the heart, guilt can keep a person in bondage indefinitely.

For almost a year after his sin with Bathsheba, David lived with the disgusting shame of a man haunted by what he had done. He was suffering, and his guilt was overwhelming. It made no difference what he did or where he went—he could not escape the awareness of his dreadful deeds and their horrible consequences. Meditate carefully on his description of the effects of his guilt:

> There is no soundness in my flesh because of thine anger; neither is there any rest in my bones because of my sin. For mine iniquities are gone over mine head: as an heavy burden they are too heavy for me. My wounds stink and are corrupt because of my foolishness. I

am troubled; I am bowed down greatly; I go mourning all the day long. For my loins are filled with a loathsome disease: and there is no soundness in my flesh. I am feeble and sore broken: I have roared by reason of the disquietness of my heart. (Ps. 38:3–8)

Though God chose David to lead Israel specifically because of his godly heart, he was still only human. Acknowledging David's fleshly nature doesn't provide an excuse for his sin; it simply states the obvious truth. David was guilty of a series of despicable sins. Lust, adultery, deceit, murder, and hypocrisy mixed with pride and arrogance to produce unbearable guilt in his tender, responsive heart. His sins were committed secretly, willingly, and without human accountability. Yet David knew what he had done, and his guilty conscience completely destroyed his peace and joy. It nearly drove him mad.

GUILT IS ESTABLISHED BY CORRUPTION

Doing right is its own reward. Even when suffering accompanies right choices (it's not unusual for those who do right to be persecuted), we can always have a sense of satisfaction for having done that which is right. David was suffering, but it wasn't because he had done the right thing. His suffering was the natural result of the guilt he was experiencing for selfish, foolish choices he made.

THE CORE OF DAVID'S SIN—PSALM 32

Though David was suffering, he had no one to blame but himself. When he finally confessed his sin, he did so by painting a solemn picture, clearly indicating the foulness of sin's nature, the twisted logic of its motivation and the train wreck it leaves behind.

> I acknowledged my sin unto thee, and mine iniquity have I not hid. I said, I will confess my transgressions unto the Lord; and thou forgavest the iniquity of my sin. (v. 5)

David's description of suffering in verses 3-4 is commonly believed to be a consequence of his sin with Bathsheba. It is clearly the result of guilt, and the details are far too specific to be considered figurative. While Psalm 32 pictures a man enjoying the blessing of forgiven sin, verse 5 powerfully describes the vile character of David's offense.

His confession covered every aspect of his wrongdoing. He acknowledged his failures openly and without qualification, taking full responsibility for his wickedness. The three words he used to refer to his sin were simple and sobering. Each one identified a different aspect of displeasing a holy God, and taken in context, they clearly reveal the cause of David's guilt.

The Measure of Sin

The first word David used referred to his sinful actions. When David said, "I acknowledged my sin unto thee," he was admitting that what he did was wrong. The word translated "sin," like its New Testament counterpart, means "to miss the mark"—to fall short of God's standard of righteousness.[13] David's inborn sinful nature prevented him from attaining a lifetime standard of righteous perfection, but in this case, David was not describing his character. Instead, he was taking the full responsibility for his actions.

The Manner of Sin

What David did was wrong, but how he did it revealed a perversion in David's thinking. David continued his confession by stating, "Mine iniquity have I not hid." The word translated "iniquity" actually means "to bend, twist, or distort."[14] It has the idea of doing things in a perverse way. David was admitting that his sin was the result of a stubborn, obstinate attitude. He was guilty not only of missing God's standard of holiness but also of twisting that standard, making it fit his corrupted opinion of what was acceptable.

The Motive for Sin

The third word David used to describe his sin was *transgressions*, which conveys the idea of "rebellion."[15] David's sin was not the result of impulse. He cautiously plotted every move, taking great care to cover his tracks. So when he said, "I will confess my transgressions unto the Lord," he was accepting responsibility for his selfish actions and acknowledging his rebellion.

THE CHARACTER OF DAVID'S SIN—2 SAMUEL 12:9-10

David's sin was far more severe than simple disobedience. He had shown contempt for God's law and scorned God's honor. Nathan used the word *despised* to characterize David's offense (v. 9). David's integrity of heart had been buried beneath his shameless pursuit of sensual gratification.

GUILT IS EXPOSED BY CONVICTION

How long can an individual conceal sin? It depends on the endurance of the individual. There are some who live for decades hiding their sin, always looking over their shoulders, wondering whether and how their sin might be exposed. Many die without ever knowing the freedom of living without guilt. David had endured the crushing burden of his guilt for almost a year before the Lord sent Nathan the prophet to confront him.

Guilt is an awareness of our responsibility for wrongdoing; conviction compels us to acknowledge it.

Nathan's purpose was not to convince David that what he did was wrong—David was intensely aware of his guilt. Instead, Nathan's role was to reveal the twisted logic that led David to justify his sin—and drive him to his knees.

GUILT IS ELIMINATED BY CONFESSION

When Nathan was finished, David had become a man with a broken spirit, a man whose only concern was that God would know of his contrition. His brief confession to Nathan (2 Sam. 12:13) was but a prelude to the heart-wrenching groans of sorrow found in Psalm 51. So deep was David's anguish of soul that his words pulsated with urgency as he sought God's forgiveness. He no longer cared about concealing his sin. His resolve to justify his sin was gone. He wanted only one thing—he longed to be reconciled to his God.

At that point everything changed. David's guilt was gone. When David's sin was *concealed*, he was miserable. His strength was failing and he could find no relief. He was dried up physically. When David's sin was *confessed*, he regained his humility. He saw his sin as an abomination before a holy God. His priorities were restored and he willingly owned up to his rebellion. When his sin was *covered* (as a result of his confession), his joy returned. He was forgiven and his guilt was gone!

AUTHENTIC REPENTANCE

It is not unusual for people to say a general prayer acknowledging their sinful nature and asking God to forgive "all their sins" and then call it repentance. Authentic repentance, however, is much more personal. It requires sobering introspection that produces specific changes in attitude and perspective.

- Authentic repentance is evidenced by complete and unconditional confession. Every ugly detail of our sin is revealed as we seek God's forgiveness. We do not attempt to hide anything.
- Authentic repentance is accompanied by an intense desire to break from the offending sin, and it will be more than getting angry that we made the mistake. We will demonstrate a passionate hatred for anything that is offensive to the God we love and desire to please.
- Authentic repentance is validated by sincere humility. In Psalm 51:17 David said, "The sacrifices of God are a broken spirit: a broken and a contrite heart, O God, thou wilt not despise." Pride will be a thing of the past, and defensiveness will vanish.

- Authentic repentance results in full and complete forgiveness. Instead of crippling guilt, we experience the healing joy and peace of complete pardon and total reconciliation.

For seven days immediately following his confession to Nathan, David fasted and prayed for the child that was born as a result of his illicit activities with Bathsheba. Although Nathan had said that the child was going to die, David maintained hope that God would in His mercy spare the child. Finally David's servants brought word that the child was indeed dead, and David resumed his normal schedule (2 Sam. 12:15–20).

While forgiveness can cleanse our hearts, restore our joy, and reconcile us to God, it can do nothing to reverse the natural results of our sinful choices. The law of sowing and reaping still applies. David was for many years privileged to live in the sunlight of God's abundant blessing. Once again, he was enjoying God's approval, but for the remainder of his life, that divine favor would be filtered by clouds of sorrow, bittersweet reminders that sin always produces unpleasant consequences.

DISCUSSION QUESTIONS

1. What is guilt? How does guilt affect an individual's life?
2. Where is sin conceived? Is it possible for people to sin without being personally responsible for their actions?
3. What can we learn from Psalm 32 about the character of sin?
4. How does guilt differ from conviction?
5. It is not unusual for people to confess their sins in a nonspecific manner, expecting God to forgive their sins. How is authentic repentance different? What attitudes display evidence of authentic repentance? What benefits are gained from authentic repentance?
6. How is forgiveness limited?

CHAPTER 14

DAVID'S GODLY HEART

TO SOME PEOPLE, SAYING THAT David had a godly heart is almost offensive. How do you apply that description to a man whose legacy includes neglecting responsibilities, lust, adultery, murder, deception, hypocrisy, and callous indifference? Saul, David's predecessor as king of Israel, was guilty of deliberate rebellion, but Scripture gives no account of him ever engaging in the kind of disgusting activity that characterized David's behavior during his sin with Bathsheba. Yet Saul, when he sought forgiveness, was rejected. What made David different?

THE SUBSTRUCTURE OF SIN

People have a natural tendency to judge others by their actions, and it is not unusual for them to form dogmatic opinions without knowing all the facts. Yet they want others to judge them by their intentions. Saul expected to be excused for his disobedience because his intentions were good. Yes, they (Saul and the people of Israel) "spared the best of the sheep and of the oxen," but their intentions were honorable; they were going to use them "to sacrifice unto the Lord" (1 Sam. 15:15). Is it even possible, however, to separate actions from intentions?

> A good man out of the good treasure of his heart bringeth forth that which is good; and an evil man out of the evil treasure of his

> heart bringeth forth that which is evil: for of the abundance of the heart his mouth speaketh. (Luke 6:45)

Jesus made this statement to His disciples as He was giving them instruction on judging others, and the danger of hypocrisy took center stage. It was common for people to condemn the sins of others while denying or excusing their own sins. The self-righteous spiritual leaders of the day (the scribes and Pharisees) were particularly guilty of such behavior, and their focus was always on appearance.

Sin, however, originates in the heart, and "the heart is deceitful above all things, and desperately wicked" (Jer. 17:9). Jesus made it clear that what people see on the outside is simply a reflection of what's in the heart.

> From within, out of the heart of men, proceed evil thoughts, adulteries, fornications, murders, thefts, covetousness, wickedness, deceit, lasciviousness, an evil eye, blasphemy, pride, foolishness. (Mark 7:21–22)

It would not be inaccurate to say that David was guilty of all the above-mentioned sins during his episode with Bathsheba, and they all originated in his heart. Saul's sin of disobedience was, likewise, conceived in his heart.

THE SIGNIFICANCE OF GOD'S AUTHORITY

Saul became king because the people demanded a king. Until then, Israel had been loosely governed by judges and prophets appointed by God—individuals whose authority was extremely limited. During those days there was no central government, no sovereign leader, and no system in place to determine the next leader. Judges, who were appointed as needed, provided leadership primarily for military challenges, and prophets relayed God's message to His people. Beyond that, individual tribes governed themselves. That was God's plan, and it worked well as long as Israel was obedient.

Israel was then at a point of decision. Samuel had "judged Israel all the days of his life" and was getting old (1 Sam. 7:15). His days as Israel's judge were numbered. Samuel prepared by appointing his sons, Joel and Abiah, to take his place (1 Sam. 8:1-2). In his mind he was showing proper concern for Israel's future, but there were problems. First, God had never provided a plan of succession for those who judged Israel. He alone made that choice according to His sovereign plan. Besides that, Samuel's sons were not qualified to lead, and the elders of Israel were painfully aware of their corruption (vv. 3-5).

Israel's response was to call a meeting with Samuel to present their demands. They would not accept Joel and Abiah as judges. Instead, they insisted that Samuel give them a king to judge them "like all the nations" (v. 5). When Samuel sought guidance from the Lord concerning his response, God authorized him to grant Israel's request. Israel's attitude was familiar. They were notorious for adopting the gods of the culture in which they lived, forsaking the true God in the process (v. 8). This was simply the latest instance of Israel rejecting God's authority over them.

Shortly after Saul was chosen, Samuel stood before all Israel to introduce them to the king God had given them. He also had a sobering message for them:

> Now therefore behold the king whom ye have chosen, and whom ye have desired! and, behold, the Lord hath set a king over you. If ye will fear the Lord, and serve him, and obey his voice, and not rebel against the commandment of the Lord, then shall both ye and also the king that reigneth over you continue following the Lord your God: But if ye will not obey the voice of the Lord, but rebel against the commandment of the Lord, then shall the hand of the Lord be against you, as it was against your fathers. (1 Sam. 12:13-15)

Samuel's warning was followed by a demonstration of God's power that left the people fearing for their lives (vv. 16-19). They were greatly convicted that asking for a king was a sin and confessed it openly.

In his warning Samuel mentioned three things that Israel—and their king—had to do if they were to enjoy God's blessing: fear the Lord, serve Him, and obey His voice. He also offered a fourth admonition, from a negative perspective—they were not to "rebel against the commandment of the Lord" (v. 14). The issues of disobedience and rebellion formed the core of Saul's downfall, and both were the result of carelessly dismissing the authority of God.

A RECKLESS KING

Saul's reign was established as a result of a sinful demand by an idolatrous people. That did not mean that Saul could not serve the Lord faithfully and have God's blessing. Indeed, his reign began on that positive note (1 Sam. 11:15). Soon, however, things started to change. As Saul became more successful, his dependence on the Lord faltered. The final reckoning came after Saul chose to ignore specific instructions concerning his battle with the Amalekites. In 1 Samuel 15 Samuel confronted him, clearly identifying Saul's sins—disobedience (v. 19) and rebellion (v. 23). Later, Samuel summarized Saul's sin when he said in verse 26, "Thou hast rejected the word of the Lord."

When Saul finally finished his attempt to justify and excuse his sin, he confessed (v. 24). At least, it sounded like a confession, but Saul's problem went much deeper. He was guilty of rejecting the word of the Lord. The word *reject* has a connotation of brazen defiance. Saul had said in principle, "I will not accept God's law as my law, nor will I accept God's will as my will." He didn't simply disobey; he totally dismissed God as his authority, displaying his insolence in the process.

Saul's life began to change. God sent Samuel to Bethlehem to anoint David as the new king of Israel. As he did, "the Spirt of the Lord came upon David" and "departed from Saul" (1 Sam. 16:13-14). Consequently, Saul's confidence began to falter. He became anxious and uncertain about his future. The Scripture says that "an evil spirit from the Lord troubled him" (v. 14). Until then, Saul's natural character had been restrained by the Spirit of God, whose presence brought peace, courage, and success. Now God's Spirit was gone, and Saul's spirit was in turmoil. Saul's heart was without question "deceitful above all things, and desperately wicked" (Jer. 17:9). By itself, Saul's heart was anything but godly, and by itself, Saul's character was clearly exposed.

- Arrogance. "Saul said, Bring hither a burnt offering to me, and peace offerings. And he offered the burnt offering" (1 Sam. 13:9). Because the battle with the Philistines was drawing near and Samuel had not yet arrived, Saul ignored the priestly order, offering his own sacrifice. He assumed that his sin would be overlooked because of his good intentions. Believing that disobedience could somehow enhance his worship was a far too common characteristic of his reign.
- Envy. "Saul was very wroth, and the saying displeased him; and he said, They have ascribed unto David ten thousands, and to me they have ascribed but thousands: and what can he have more but the kingdom?" (1 Sam. 18:8). David had become one of Saul's most trusted soldiers. Not only was he fighting on Saul's behalf; he was also commanding his troops and doing a superb job (v. 5). As a result, David was well favored by the people and received widespread acclaim. Saul, who no longer had God's approval, was fearful of losing the confidence of the people as well. He began to view David as his rival, assuming he was attempting to steal the throne.
- Cruelty. The fact that Saul was a cruel man is undeniable. On one occasion he was determined to slay his own son Jonathan for violating an oath he had made forbidding any man to eat food before evening. Jonathan was indeed guilty of violating the oath, but he did so in ignorance, and it was obvious that he

didn't agree with his father's policies (1 Sam. 14:24-30). When Saul learned that someone was guilty, he made another vow, one that showed grave disrespect for the Lord: "As the LORD liveth, which saveth Israel, though it be in Jonathan my son, he shall surely die" (v. 39). Yet Jonathan didn't die. Israel sided with Jonathan, citing his victorious efforts in the battle, leaving Saul to deal with his shattered pride (vv. 45-46). Later, Saul again tried to kill Jonathan, casting his javelin at him for defending David (1 Sam. 20:33).

- Violence. David was a loyal servant to Saul. Because the Spirit of God was guiding him, he was both prosperous in his military endeavors and popular with the people (1 Sam. 18:5). Neither of those characteristics was positive in Saul's eyes. It is not unusual for suspicious people to assume others think as they do, so Saul assumed David was trying to steal the throne and determined that he would use any means necessary to defeat his "enemy." Three times Saul tried to spear David with his javelin (1 Sam. 18:11; 19:10). Then he devised a plan by which David would be left to die at the hand of the enemy, demanding evidence of the death of one hundred Philistines for his daughter's hand in marriage (1 Sam. 18:25). When that plan failed, he sent assassins to David's house to slay him (1 Sam. 19:11). For about ten years he personally pursued David to kill him. Violence was simply his way of settling the score.
- Vindictiveness. Saul's interest in pursuing David was not driven by a concern for his welfare. Saul was bent on putting David in his place, making sure he would never occupy the throne of Israel, and seeing that he was punished. It had nothing to do with honoring God and everything to do with satisfying his thirst for revenge.
- Impenitence. Though Saul confessed his sin, it was obvious that he didn't repent. Samuel's final condemnation came *after* Saul's confession. Samuel said to Saul, "Thou hast rejected the

word of the Lord, and the Lord hath rejected thee from being king over Israel" (1 Sam. 15:26). Since repentance requires that an individual *accept* the word of the Lord, we must conclude that Saul's confession fell short. He acknowledged that his actions displeased the Lord, but there is no clear evidence that he accepted the validity of God's claim on his life.

A FAITHFUL SHEPHERD

David's career began in the field caring for his father's sheep. He was the youngest of eight boys in the family, and he was treated accordingly. Consequently, people didn't look up to him or expect great things from him. Nor did such a life encourage egotistical speculation regarding future employment. Even after Samuel anointed him king of Israel, he seems to have had no visions of grandeur or elevated sense of importance. David's spirit continued to be firmly anchored by humility and submission. His only concern was to be faithful in the job he had been given, so he continued to care for the sheep.

As his life unfolded, David faced many significant challenges—situations that would normally provoke turmoil. Opposition from his brother over his desire to fight Goliath, a schizophrenic king who displayed affection one minute and then morphed into a mad killer the next, and constant uncertainty regarding his immediate status in Israel's government would be enough to unravel any man's security. Yet David never flinched. Two things encouraged his steadfastness in the face of absolute chaos—he had unfailing faith in the promise and purpose of God, and he knew that his God was in control. The character of David's heart was the categorical opposite of the king he was seeking to serve and destined to replace.

- Commitment. "David said, What have I now done? Is there not a cause?" (1 Sam. 17:29). David's actions were generally dictated by principles of righteousness. Feelings had little impact. He responded to the challenge of Goliath not because Goliath had personally insulted him but because he had obviously disrespected Israel's God. The trained soldiers of Israel's army focused on Goliath's size and strength, which was enough to cause any man to falter. David, however, disregarded the very real possibility of death. Only one thing mattered—the blasphemy had to stop.

- Courage. David's principles would mean little without courage. David did more than boldly state an opinion; he backed it up with his actions. David won the battle against Goliath because he refused to be intimidated by the giant. He won because he refused to allow the giant to dictate the rules of the game. He won because he refused to allow his fear to control him. Faith produces confidence not in personal wisdom or ability but in the power of God. Men who are naturally incapable of facing the challenges set before them overcome them because of the courage produced by their faith. David had such courage, because of his trust in God.
- Grace. One of Saul's requests of David, when he was thinking properly, was that once he became king, David would treat his family with compassion (1 Sam. 24:20-21). In the event of a revolution, it was standard procedure for a newly installed king to begin his reign by purging the kingdom of all family members of the previous ruler. Fulfilling that promise was easy for David because he loved Saul and his family. The Bible portrays David's heart-wrenching grief over the deaths of Saul and Jonathan with great candor (2 Sam. 1:19-27).

David's opportunity to fulfill his vow did not occur until well after Israel and Judah were finally united under his reign. Second Samuel 9 gives the details. David inquired concerning any surviving family members of the house of Saul. When he learned that a son of Jonathan still lived in Lodebar, he sent for him. "He was five years old when the tidings came of Saul and Jonathan out of Jezreel, and his nurse took him up, and fled: and it came to pass, as she made haste to flee, that he fell, and became lame. And his name was Mephibosheth" (2 Sam. 4:4).

When Mephibosheth arrived, David treated him with Christlike grace. He first returned to Mephibosheth all the property that had belonged to his grandfather Saul. He gave him a permanent seat to take his meals at the royal table and made him master over Ziba, Saul's servant, who had fifteen sons and twenty servants of his own. Indeed, David returned good for bad, fulfilling his vow to Saul as well as his good friend Jonathan.

- Humility. "Then went king David in, and sat before the LORD, and he said, Who am I, O Lord God? and what is my house, that thou hast brought me hitherto?" (2 Sam. 7:18). At this point David had finally realized the fulfillment of Samuel's prophecy; he was king of a united Israel. His first concern was to restore formal worship among the people. It was a good idea, but formal worship was impossible without access to the ark, which was in the house of Abinadab in Gibeah (2 Sam. 6:3). Though it took two attempts, David eventually succeeded in bringing the ark to Jerusalem, and he lodged it in a tent that he had pitched for that purpose (v. 17). When David expressed a desire to build a proper home for the ark, God sent the prophet Nathan to David with another message, a covenant promise to the king that was more wonderful than he could have ever imagined. It included a commitment by God to allow David's son to build a permanent home for the ark; a promise that God would treat David's heir as His son, chastening him when he sinned but never removing His mercy from him;

and a pledge that David's house, kingdom, and throne would be established forever (2 Sam. 7:8–17).

David's response was not that of a self-sufficient monarch. Unlike Saul, he knew the source of his prosperity, and he was too smart to take credit for what God had done. He responded instead with the humility of a faithful servant whose sole concern was honoring his master.

- Faith. Patience as a virtue seldom stands alone. It is usually paired with some spiritual challenge that serves to validate and strengthen the discipline necessary for its exercise. Effective leadership requires patience. Personal growth requires patience. Enduring tribulation requires patience. In David's case it was seeing God's plan and purpose fulfilled in his life that required him to exercise patience. In every case, however, patience is a consequence of unconditional faith in God.

David's reign as king of Israel was a long time coming, and I am sure there were times when David got weary of waiting. If the promise David was clinging to had been made by a man, he would have abandoned it years earlier. But it wasn't. God had chosen him, and it was David's responsibility to serve faithfully while he waited.

David spent years fleeing from Saul, who was consumed with a desire to kill him. Undoubtedly, David would have been justified in defending himself, and I'm sure there were many occasions when he felt a strong compulsion to take that step. Instead, he chose to wait patiently for God to move Saul out of the way as He saw fit.

- Contrition. Repentance requires more than a simple statement acknowledging responsibility for error. That was Saul's approach, and it left him without pardon. There must be, in the heart of the penitent, an overwhelming awareness of the magnitude of the offense coupled with a clear understanding of the need for mercy. David's agonizing plea for cleansing in Psalm 51 is a perfect example of genuine repentance. The focus of his prayer is found in verses 16–17: "Thou desirest not sacrifice; else would I give it: thou delightest not in burnt offering. The sacrifices of God are a broken spirit: a broken and a contrite heart, O God, thou wilt not despise."

The Hebrew word translated "contrite" is used five times in Scripture, and verse 17 is the only time it is translated "contrite." Once we find the word "croucheth" (Ps. 10:10), and three times it is rendered "broken" (Ps. 38:8; 44:19; 51:8). It is the Hebrew word *dakah*, which means "to crush."[16]

Genuine contrition is characterized by a crippling sense of guilt, unqualified humility, and total helplessness. There is no concern for maintaining dignity or pride, and spiritual purity becomes the primary objective. In every case where David was confronted with his transgression, he responded with deep contrition of heart and a singular desire to be reconciled to God.

That attitude of contrition is by far the greatest evidence of David's godly heart. He was not perfect, and he often found it necessary to acknowledge his failures. Like the apostle Paul, his flesh often hindered his desire to do the right thing (Rom. 7:14–25). But David's confessions were complete and honest, always taking full responsibility for his sin. At no time did he ever attempt to justify or excuse his sin.

A godly heart does not require sinless perfection. It does require simple, sincere integrity. David's life was characterized by such integrity. It is the primary reason that David, a sinful man, is said to have a godly heart.

DISCUSSION QUESTIONS

1. What argument did Saul offer as an excuse for sparing the best of the sheep and the oxen in direct disobedience to God's clear command?
2. How do actions and intentions relate to each other? Is it possible to separate actions from intentions?
3. Where does sin originate? What is the natural condition of man's heart?
4. What two issues formed the core of Saul's collapse as king of Israel? What did those issues reveal about Saul's relationship with God?
5. In 1 Samuel 15:24 Saul made a statement that sounds like a confession. But confession requires more than simply acknowledging a transgression. What was lacking in Saul's "confession"?
6. How did Saul's posture change when the Lord withdrew His Spirit from Saul?
7. What was Saul's natural character—unrestrained by God's Spirit—really like?
8. How was David's character different from that of Saul?

CONCLUSION
THE SOURCE OF GODLINESS

DAVID REIGNED OVER JUDAH AND Israel for forty years. His life was not perfect. He made mistakes, some of which were significant. He also experienced many remarkable victories. Yet David never forgot where he got his strength and who was responsible for the success he enjoyed.

Psalm 37 provides a fitting description of David's understanding of the Lord's guidance and blessing in his life: He walked with God, always trusting the Lord to order his steps (v. 23). Though he did on many occasions fall, he was never "utterly cast down: for the Lord [upheld] him with his hand" (v. 24). He was keenly aware that the Lord is "ever merciful" and that He "forsaketh not his saints" (vv. 26, 28). He understood the importance of waiting on God and knew from experience that the "salvation of the righteous is of the Lord" (v. 39).

David's story is not about his accomplishments, his victories, or his faithfulness. Nor is it about his godliness. It's about David's dependence on his God and God's willingness to use him in spite of his human weaknesses. If we learn anything from David's life, it is that David's godly heart was not the result of his character. Instead, it was a consequence of David's awareness of his ungodly character.

The essential truth is that genuine godliness is possible only when we realize that it is impossible without God's help. David clearly understood that principle. His life reflected that understanding, and his example is a challenge to every believer.

ENDNOTES

1. C. H. Spurgeon, *The Treasury of David*, vol. 2 (Peabody, MA: Hendrickson, 1988), 239.
2. Spurgeon, Treasury of David, 240.
3. F. B. Meyer, *David: Shepherd, Psalmist, King* (New York: Fleming H. Revell, 1895), 36.
4. Matthew Henry, *Matthew Henry's Concise Commentary on the Whole Bible* (Nashville, TN: Thomas Nelson, 1997), 454.
5. C. F. Keil and F. Delitzsch, *Commentary on the Old Testament*, vol. 2 (Peabody, MA: Hendrickson, 1996), 485.
6. Shakespeare, *Othello*, ed. Barbara A. Mowat and Paul Werstine (New York: Simon & Schuster, 2017), 3.3.195–97.
7. Warren Wiersbe, *Be Successful (1 Samuel): Attaining Wealth That Money Can't Buy* (Colorado Springs, CO: David C Cook, 2001), 153.
8. C. F. Keil and F. Delitzsch, *Commentary on the Old Testament*, vol. 2 (Peabody, MA: Hendrickson, 1996), 526.
9. M. G. Easton, *Illustrated Bible Dictionary*, 3rd ed. (Nashville, Thomas Nelson: 1897), s.v. "Helkath-hazzurim," www.biblestudytools.com/dictionary/helkath-hazzurim.
10. C. F. Keil and F. Delitzsch, *Commentary on the Old Testament*, vol. 2 (Peabody, MA: Hendrickson, 1996), 568.
11. Alfred Edersheim, *Israel under Samuel, Saul, and David, to the Birth of Solomon* (Grand Rapids, MI: Eerdmans, n.d.), 157.

12. *American Heritage*, s.v. "complacency," accessed September 7, 2018, https://ahdictionary.com/word/search.html?q=complacency.
13. Blue Letter Bible, s.v. *"chatta'ath,"* accessed September 8, 2018, www.blueletterbible.org/lang/lexicon/lexicon.cfm?Strongs=H2403&t=KJV; Blue Letter Bible, s.v. *"hamartia,"* accessed September 8, 2018, www.blueletterbible.org/lang/lexicon/lexicon.cfm?t=kjv&strongs=g266.
14. Blue Letter Bible, s.v. *"`avon,"* accessed September 8, 2018, www.blueletterbible.org/lang/lexicon/lexicon.cfm?Strongs=H5771&t=KJV; Blue Letter Bible, s.v. *"`avah,"* accessed September 8, 2018, www.blueletterbible.org/lang/lexicon/lexicon.cfm?strongs=H5753&t=KJV.
15. Blue Letter Bible, s.v. *"pesha`,"* accessed September 8, 2018, www.blueletterbible.org/lang/lexicon/lexicon.cfm?Strongs=H6588&t=KJV.
16. Blue Letter Bible, s.v. *"dakah,"* accessed September 9, 2018, www.blueletterbible.org/lang/lexicon/lexicon.cfm?Strongs=H1794&t=KJV.

ABOUT THE AUTHOR

TERRY HYMAN PASTORED TRINITY BAPTIST Church in Centerville, Georgia, for almost twenty-one years. His ministry spans more than forty-eight years and includes a number of churches throughout the southeast. He is the author of *Studies in the Minor Prophets*, written to help church members understand and apply the eternal truths found in those "uninteresting" and "impractical" prophecies, and he posts often at www.terryhyman.net. He and his wife, Myra, have three sons and ten grandchildren.

For more information about
Terry Hyman
and
David
please visit:

www.terryhyman.net
@pastortwhyman
www.linkedin.com/in/terry-hyman-68016843

Ambassador International's mission is to magnify the Lord Jesus Christ and promote His Gospel through the written word.

We believe through the publication of Christian literature, Jesus Christ and His Word will be exalted, believers will be strengthened in their walk with Him, and the lost will be directed to Jesus Christ as the only way of salvation.

For more information about
AMBASSADOR INTERNATIONAL
please visit:

www.ambassador-international.com

@AmbassadorIntl

www.facebook.com/AmbassadorIntl

Thank you for reading this book. Please consider leaving us a review on your social media, favorite retailer's website, Goodreads or Bookbub, or our website.

MORE FROM AMBASSADOR INTERNATIONAL

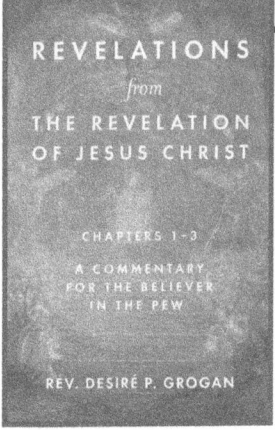

The purpose of this commentary is to empower you—the believer in the pew—with the most accessible tool to navigate and understand this last Book of Scripture, and that tool is the Bible itself, the Bible in your hand!

In this powerful work, Dr. Wiles shares eighteen insights for learning how to pray, handle our anger, love our enemies, overcome worry, have a healthy marriage, and so much more. Included are questions for personal reflection or group discussions. *Don't Just Live . . . Really Live* offers a practical approach for discerning how to live out the Bible in today's world.

Within the foundations of despair and hopelessness is the cry, "Can someone help me? Can someone call on God for me?" God is not deaf to the cries of this generation—He created you with this generation in mind. He is counting on you to step out and meet the needs of this day and age. He has equipped you for the difficult times ahead. Allow God to guide and to work through you. Display His splendor to those around you.

www.ingramcontent.com/pod-product-compliance
Lightning Source LLC
Chambersburg PA
CBHW070453100426
42743CB00010B/1604